PLUGGED

—INTO—

GOD

the ultimate power source

LAWRENCE P. LUBY

HIS Publishing Group
4310 Wiley Post Rd., Suite 201D
Addison, TX 75001
info@hispub.com

ISBN-13:   978-1-7352651-3-1 *paperback*
                978-1-7352651-4-8 *ebook*

Library of Congress Control Number: 2021949980

Plugged Into God – The Ultimate Power Source
Summary: "God is the ultimate power source, so like Jesus, when we *plug into God,* we have access to a supernatural source of power and are protected from spiritually short-circuiting." —Provided by the publisher.

1. Religion 2. Spiritual life 3. Inspirational

Printed in the United States of America
10 9 8 7 6 5 4 3 2 1

HISPUBLISHING
GROUP
Division of Human Improvement Specialists, llc.
www.hispubg.com | *info@hispubg.com*

DEDICATION

To Judy, my loving and joyful wife.

To our son Casey, our son Kyle and his wife Sarah Jo
and our grandchildren Mary Owen and Jane Carson.

I am also grateful for my spiritual family who
took the time to read through and
offer suggestions: Betty and Jim Siber, Liz and
Pat Sibley, Rt. Rev. Philip Jones

CONTENTS

INTRODUCTION

GOD'S POWER STRIP

"For since the creation of the world His invisible attributes are clearly seen, being understood by the things that are made, even His eternal power and Godhead, so that they are without excuse." (Romans 1:20)

We all know what a power strip is, that wonderful device which allows us to plug a variety of our electronics into a single source. The power strip serves two unique purposes. It gives us access to one source of power, and it protects us from electrical surges that cause damage to our computers and other precious electronics.

We work with sources of power every day, and the source of that power is usually hidden from our view. For example, when we turn on our coffeemaker in the morning, we see the cord plugged into the wall, but we do not see the current flow to the pot. We flip a switch on the wall, and the lights come on, but we do not see the source of the power. Most items we use today are wireless, but without power they will not operate. They, too, must be plugged into a power source, into power we cannot see but readily accept.

For years, we have been infatuated with stories about the supernatural. These stories appeal to us because somewhere deep inside our being, we long to tap into a supreme power source. We desire a power source that can provide an unlimited source of energy. We read stories about supernatural characters that all contain some secret source of power.

Did you see the movie *Iron Man*? Robert Downey Jr. plays Tony Stark, a billionaire industrialist who inherited the family business, Stark Enterprise, a renowned defense contractor. Stark develops an incredible device drawing on a magnetic power source that gives him supernatural abilities. The movie makes the following point, "Just think, if we could harness that kind of power, the world would never be the same."

It is a fact that the world's main source of energy is the sun. We have been plugging into its energy as a source of power since the beginning of time.

> *The primary source of energy to the Earth is radiant energy from the sun. This radiant energy is measured and reported as the solar irradiance. When all of the radiation is measured, collectively, it is called the Total Solar Irradiance (TSI). When measured as a function of wavelength, it is the spectral irradiance. Light of different wavelengths reaches different parts of the Earth's atmosphere. Visible light and infrared radiation reach the surface, warming the surface to livable conditions.[1]*

For generations, man has longed to tap into the power of the universe because he who has the most power ultimately has the most control in the natural world.

There are sources of power in existence today that are hidden and must be searched out. For example, back in 1998, scientists discovered that there was an incredible energy source in the universe and named it "Dark Energy."

> *A web of interlocking observations has established that the expansion of the Universe is speeding up and not slowing, thereby revealing the presence of some form of repulsive gravity. Within the context of general relativity, the cause of cosmic acceleration is a highly elastic (p~-ρ), very smooth form of energy called "dark energy," accounts for about 75% of the Universe. The simplest*

---

1   https://www.nasa.gov/mission_pages/sdo/science/solar-irradiance.html

explanation for dark energy is the zero-point energy density associated with the quantum vacuum; however, all estimates for its value are many orders-of-magnitude too large. Other ideas for dark energy include a very light scalar field or a tangled network of topological defects. An alternate explanation invokes gravitational physics beyond general relativity. Observations and experiments underway, and more precise cosmological measurements and laboratory experiments planned for the next decade will test whether or not dark energy is the quantum energy of the vacuum or something more exotic and whether or not general relativity can consistently self explain cosmic acceleration. Dark energy is the most conspicuous example of physics beyond the standard model, and perhaps the most profound mystery in all of science.[2]

It is interesting to think that it took us until 1998 to discover that there is an enormous power that makes up 75% of our known universe. However, that is just what we know. The universe is growing at a rate unfathomable to man and is being propelled by energy we do not understand and cannot control. Is it any wonder the scientist named it *Dark Energy*?

Naturally, one might think that tapping into this kind of power source would eliminate the debate about our future energy needs and would put an end to our dependency on foreign oil. However, man's way of thinking about power is physical, but I want to suggest a spiritual way of thinking about it.

---

2   https://ui.adsabs.harvard.edu/abs/2007JPSJ...76k1015T/abstract

THOUGHT PROVOKING

I ask you to consider, is it possible there is a power source available to us all that fuels not only dark energy, but also every living thing?

God is the ultimate power source, so like Jesus, when we *plug into God,* we have access to a supernatural source of power and are protected from spiritually short-circuiting.

Jesus was born plugged into the Father's power strip, but He knew in order to draw power from the Father, spending time in prayer, usually in solitude, was important. Because we are made in the Father's image, He longs for us to spend time with Him. As parents we can relate. How many of us long for our children to spend time with us?

God's power is not something to be grasped for physical gain. His power is spiritual and is much stronger than any physical power we can imagine. Consider the following statements made by Jesus in Matthew about our lack of understanding concerning the power of God.

Matthew 17:20

"So Jesus said to them, 'Because of your unbelief; for assuredly, I say to you, if you have faith as a mustard seed, you will say to this mountain, 'Move from here to there,' and it will move; and nothing will be impossible for you.'"

Matthew 22:29

"Jesus answered and said to them, "You are mistaken, not knowing the Scriptures nor the power of God."

In James we learn that our prayers are necessary for healing. There is power in prayer because we connect to the source which is God the Father, God the Son, and God the Holy Spirit.

James 5:16-18

"Confess your trespasses to one another and pray for one another, that you may be healed. The effective, fervent prayer of a righteous man avails much. Elijah was a man with a nature like ours, and he prayed earnestly that it would not rain; and it did not rain on the land for three years and six months. And he prayed again, and the heaven gave rain, and the earth produced its fruit."

For a moment allow your mind to be open to a supernatural way of thinking and imagine that God is like one of our physical power strips. However, because His power strip is spiritual, He can accept an infinite number of plug-ins, plug-ins that extend from and are attached to every living thing in the world.

From scripture we learn that God can be anywhere at any time (Omnipresent), is all-powerful (Omnipotent), and is all-knowing (Omniscient).

God is Omnipresent – Present in all places at the same time, ubiquitous, as the omnipresent Jehovah.

Psalm 139:7-12

"Where can I go from Your Spirit? Or where can I flee from Your presence? If I ascend into heaven, You are there; If I make my bed in hell, behold, You are there. If I take the wings of the morning, and dwell in the uttermost parts of the sea, even there Your hand shall lead me, And Your right hand shall hold me. If I say, "Surely the darkness shall fall on me," even the night shall be light about me. Indeed, the darkness shall not hide from You, but the night shines as the day; The darkness and the light are both alike to You."

God is Omnipotent – Able in every respect and for every work; unlimited in ability; all-powerful; almighty.

Jeremiah 32:17-18

"Ah, Lord GOD! Behold, You have made the heavens and the earth by Your great power and outstretched arm. There is nothing too hard for You. You show lovingkindness to thousands and repay the iniquity of the fathers into the bosom of their children after them—the Great, the Mighty God, whose name is the LORD of hosts."

God is Omniscient – Having universal knowledge; knowing all things; infinitely knowing or wise; as, the omniscient God.

Psalm 147:5

"Great is our Lord, and mighty in power; His understanding is infinite."

With this knowledge, would it not make sense to believe that everything we know and the things we have yet to discover are plugged into God's power strip? Thus, everyone and everything has the potential to be connected to one another through God, the ultimate power source. God's power strip never fills up.

Jeremiah 51:15

"He has made the earth by His power; He has established the world by His wisdom, and stretched out the heaven by His understanding."

By His grace, He allows us to unplug from the world. Then, as we plug into God's power strip through being *Born Again*, His Holy Spirit enters our hearts and begins to work from the inside out, changing us, molding us, and re-creating us into His image. He ushers us into a loving relationship with Him. He longs to wash us clean through water baptism and ignite our spirit through the baptism of His Holy Spirit, which we will explore in detail in Chapter Six. Thus, we become part of His spiritual family/Kingdom.

John 3:5-8

"Jesus answered and said to him, 'Most assuredly, I say to you, unless one is born again, he cannot see the kingdom of God.' Nicodemus said to Him, 'How can a man be born when he is old? Can he enter a second time into his mother's womb and be born?' Jesus answered, 'Most assuredly, I say to you, unless one is born of water and the Spirit, he cannot enter the kingdom of God. That which is born of the flesh is flesh, and that which is born of the Spirit is spirit. Do not marvel that I said to you, 'You must be born again.' The wind blows where it wishes, and you hear the sound of it, but cannot tell where it comes from and where it goes. So is everyone who is born of the Spirit.'"

As we embrace His Word and believe in Him as the true power source, we escape judgement and have assurance of an everlasting life.

John 5:24

"Most assuredly, I say to you, he who hears My word and believes in Him who sent Me has everlasting life and shall not come into judgment, but has passed from death into life."

He continues to instruct us so that we will stay plugged into His power. He connects us to other believers who are also plugged into His power strip. These relationships give us strength for our walk.

Matthew 5:1-10

> *And seeing the multitudes, He went up on a mountain, and when He was seated His disciples came to Him. Then, He opened His mouth and taught them, saying, "Blessed are the poor in spirit, for theirs is the kingdom of heaven. Blessed are those who mourn, for they shall be comforted. Blessed are the meek, for they shall inherit earth. Blessed are those who hunger and thirst for righteousness, for they shall be filled. Blessed are the merciful, for they shall obtain mercy. Blessed are the pure in heart, for they shall see God. Blessed are the peacemakers, for they shall be called sons of God. Blessed are those who are persecuted for righteousness' sake, for theirs is the kingdom of heaven.*

Like the secular power strips that protect us from surges, God's power strip provides protection from sin's surges that mean to do us harm. He empowers us to live righteously and desires that we would embrace His peace and joy.

CHALLENGE QUESTIONS

Who created dark energy?

How did Jesus tap into God's eternal power source?

Who can plug into God's power strip?

What things around us are plugged into God's power strip?

What does it mean for a Christian to be *Born Again*?

Discuss what could be accomplished if Christians embraced the concept of Plugging into God.

CHAPTER I

❧

DANGER OF NOT PLUGGING INTO GOD

"Or do you not know that your body is the temple of the Holy Spirit who is in you, whom you have from God, and you are not your own? For you were bought at a price; therefore, glorify God in your body and in your spirit, which are God's." (1 Corinthians 6:19-20)

The danger of not plugging into God's power source is missing the opportunity for a personal relationship with the Father. Of course, the most unfortunate consequence would be dying and living an eternity separated from Him.

Sin desires us to plug into one another outside the covering of God. If you do not believe this statement, just look all around you at the liberal media broadcasting from billboards, radio, television, movies, Internet, and social media. Immoral sex is rampant, lust is promoted, and self-control is non-existent. Alcohol and drugs are being consumed on a gigantic scale. People are becoming infected with all kinds of viruses, with AIDS being one of the most prolific.

I have a good friend who confided in me about some people she knows. They are married couples who meet on a regular basis and trade partners. Her female friends tell her they are so depressed and ashamed, but they don't see a way out. Their husbands have drawn them into a satanic world where unity cannot co-exist. Their lives will be forever impacted, and without Christ, their marriages are doomed, and their families will be divided.

THOUGHT PROVOKING

What will happen to their children?

These behaviors are happening everywhere in the world today. Unfortunately, it is happening even in our churches here in America. No one is immune to the carcinoma of sin that has **metastasized in our societal systems.** I challenge that the main reason our systems are infected is due to our ignorance of the spiritual erosion sin inflicts. I ask, are you content to sit idly by and watch further erosion? If not, what is your solution for the sin that has inculcated our society?

In the natural body, the lymph nodes are the gateway into your system, and once a cancer has reached these nodes, you have no choice but to start a treatment program to eradicate the cancer. The cancer cells disguise themselves as normal cells. The sentinel node, or the first lymph node to which extracellular fluid from a tumor drains, acts as the gateway to the lymphatic system and beyond.[3]

Sin is a form of cancer, a deceptive and destructive force the Satan (enemy) has used to destroy our bodily temples. It is in direct opposition to the Spirit that longs to dwell in us. Like in the human body, the cancer of sin has reached the sentinel node and has infected and spread within our societal system for generations, disguising itself through subtle deception as a normal and natural part of our societal, cellular makeup. To help make this point, let me share an experience.

In 1990, I was a member of an Episcopal church in one of the grandest cities in Texas. It had a membership exceeding 4,000 people. I attended a men's group led by one of the priests. We met on a weekly basis to share God's word and press into the Lord. At one of those meetings, a member asked the priest if it was all right for two people to have consensual sex outside of marriage. The priest did not hesitate in his response and said, "Of course, between two responsible adults." Where in the Holy

---

3   http://www2.mdanderson.org/depts/onco-
     log/articles/03/9-sep/9-03-1.html

Scriptures could he possibly support such a response? The Bible is specific on this topic.

Hebrews 13:4

> *"Marriage is honorable among all and the bed undefiled, but fornicators and adulterers God will judge."*

He went on to tell a tale of a woman he was dating: "As I was preaching from the pulpit, my girlfriend was sitting in one of the front rows flirting with me, and I could hardly preach my sermon. After the service, we could not wait to reach her home. As soon as we hit the door, clothes started flying, but as I went to remove my collar, she stopped me. At that moment, I realized she wanted to make love to the collar not to me, so I immediately left her house."

Take a moment and let his story sink in! Unbelievable is all that comes to mind as I reflect on that story. Regardless, if he were wearing a collar or not, he was in the wrong place with the wrong person and was putting himself and his congregation at risk.

You may be thinking, "He was either an idiot, unschooled, or deceived." Well, he was educated, and I can tell you he was not an idiot by definition, so that only leaves deceived.

His response was not the sad part of this story. The sad part about this story is that not one man, including myself, stood up and brought a biblical rebuke. No, instead we all asked where we could sign up for his club. What single adult male, if truthful, would not want that kind of approval? Especially from his priest.

Why do you think Jihad is so popular among young Muslim men? They have been deceived into carrying out "martyrdom operations" for Islam, for in Islam you must earn a place in paradise. They have been brainwashed into believing that by spilling their blood in holy war they will be guaranteed a place in paradise.

In contrast, as Christians, all we must do to gain paradise is place our trust in Jesus Christ. Unfortunately, many are ignorant to the deception of the flesh and are all too willing to buy into the lies when the outcome appears enticing.

Currently within the Christian community, sin has many conditioned into thinking that pre-marital sex between responsible adults is okay. In the case of our group, who was defining our moral code, God or man? Based on our sick understanding at the time, we were sent out and held accountable to the wrong moral code.

Matthew 18:6

> *"But whoever causes one of these little ones who believe in Me to sin, it would be better for him if a millstone were hung around his neck, and he were drowned in the depth of the sea."*

Let us not judge the priest in this story because he was only a pawn. I am sure God has already dealt with his heart. However, make no mistake about it, he was plugged into the wrong power source. The deceiver was his flesh. The cancer of sin had reached his spiritual lymph nodes and was spreading throughout his system, threatening to infect everyone with whom he came into contact.

THOUGHT PROVOKING

If we do not make a conscious decision to plug into God before death, how could we expect to live in eternity plugged into Him? Have we become ignorant to the state of our spiritual health?

The answer is found in Matthew 7:21-23,

> *"Not everyone who says to Me, 'Lord, Lord,' shall enter the kingdom of heaven, but he who does the will of My Father in heaven. Many will say to Me in that day, 'Lord, Lord, have we not prophesied in Your name, cast out demons in Your name, and done many wonders in Your name?' And then I will declare to them, 'Depart from me. I never knew you. Depart from Me, you who practice lawlessness!'"*

When we are not plugged into God, we are in essence walking in disobedience to His word. Jesus Christ reveals the truth to us through the Holy Spirit, so unless we are plugged into His body and blood through the belief of His sacrifice on the cross, we run the risk of allowing the enemy of sin to infiltrate our spiritual systems and spread throughout.

Ephesians 2:1-3

"And you He made alive, who were dead in trespasses and sins, in which you once walked according to the course of this world, according to the prince of the power of the air, the spirit who now works in the sons of disobedience, among whom also we all once conducted ourselves in the lusts of our flesh, fulfilling the desires of the flesh and of the mind, and were by nature children of wrath, just as the others."

CHALLENGE QUESTIONS

What is the danger of not plugging into God's power source?

How can sin be compared to cancer?

In your inner circle, who is defining your moral code?

Do you have your moral values written down?

Have you shared those values with your children?

Discuss what living an eternity plugged into God might look like.

CHAPTER II

PLUGGED INTO OTHERS OUTSIDE OF GOD'S WILL

"Do not love the world or the things in the world. If anyone loves the world, the love of the Father is not in him. For all that is in the world—the lust of the flesh, the lust of the eyes, and the pride of life—is not of the Father but is of the world. And the world is passing away, and the lust of it, but he who does the will of God abides forever." (1 John 2:15-17)

Think of the way society has prompted us to plug into others outside of God's will. We plug into unhealthy spiritual relationships when we follow false doctrines not supported by scripture. We plug into one another physically through sexual intercourse outside of marriage. We plug into one another in our personal relationships by giving another person power over our emotions.

Without realizing it, in the spiritual realm, we have become joined with those people and the people they previously have plugged into outside of God's will.

1 Corinthians 6:15-16

> *"Do you not know that your bodies are members of
> Christ? Shall I then take the members of Christ and
> make them members of a harlot? Certainly not! Or
> do you not know that he who is joined to a harlot
> is one body with her? For 'the two,' He says, 'shall
> become one flesh.'"*

The harlot referred to here is not just a prostitute. It is anyone or anything that is being used by the enemy to lure you into an unhealthy spiritual, physical, or emotional union before plugging into God's power strip. The practice of idolatry lures you away from a pure relationship with God.

Many people desire and need affection to feel loved. Oftentimes, they become so emotionally starved they will give themselves sexually in order to obtain that affection or love. Sometimes, they submit because they are afraid of upsetting or possibly losing the other person. Or they might be unknowingly trying to replace a lost love or possibly the love of a parent.

What they do not realize is that they are exposing their hearts to the other person. Based on that person's agenda, they may be putting themselves in a vulnerable position. If they have entered an unhealthy, physical relationship, then they have also entered an unhealthy emotional and spiritual relationship and risk being trapped in an unhealthy, spiritual state controlled by a spiritual enemy.

THOUGHT PROVOKING

*Why do you think we are encouraged to abstain from sex prior
to marriage?*

When you abstain for spiritual protection, your heart is more protected and not as easily impacted by any deceptive emotions the other person may have. Abstinence provides a protective covering that allows more time to get to know the true nature of one another's heart. If the relationship does not work out, you most likely still experience emotional pain, but to a lesser degree than if you had been physically involved in the relationship.

The cultures we live and work in have set us up to block God's blessing over our lives. By abstaining from sex before marriage, you plug into God's intention for the marriage bed to be undefiled so that two would be made one in the power of His Spirit.

Matthew 19:4-6

"And He answered and said to them, 'Have you not read that He who made them at the beginning 'made them male and female,' and said, 'For this reason a man shall leave his father and mother and be joined to his wife, and the two shall become one flesh'? So then, they are no longer two but one flesh. Therefore, what God has joined together, let not man separate.'"

How can I make the claim that plugging into a sexual relationship outside of God is blocking God's blessing? Think about it: if God is a righteous judge and a loving Father, how can He bless a relationship that is committing a sinful act? Would He not be defeating himself? Would He not be blessing the very thing that is keeping you out of a right relationship with Him?

Mark 3:25

"And if a house is divided against itself, that house cannot stand."

God wants a personal relationship with each and every one of us. The relationship with Him is not going to blossom if we are plugged into another person physically, spiritually, or emotionally outside of His will. God is a jealous God.

Exodus 34:13-15

"But you shall destroy their altars, break their sacred pillars, and cut down their wooden images (for you

shall worship no other god, for the LORD, whose name is Jealous, is a jealous God), lest you make a covenant with the inhabitants of the land, and they play the harlot with their gods and make sacrifice to their gods, and one of them invites you and you eat of his sacrifice,"

Oprah Winfrey once stated on her show, "When I was a young girl and heard that God was a jealous God, something did not sit right with me." If Oprah had been directed to look up the scripture, she might have gained a different perspective. "Lest you make a covenant with the inhabitants of the land, and they play the harlot with their gods." Could it be that God loves us so much that He is not going to compete with evil forces that are out to destroy our souls? Instead, he is jealous in a good sense, in his love for us. He longs to provide protection from the sins that so easily entrap us.

God is not human, so His jealousy is void of sin, unlike our human jealousy. His jealousy is grounded in His unconditional love. He longs to have a pure relationship with us.

If you do know Christ and you have plugged into another person physically through intercourse, and you are asking God to bless the relationship, then you are asking him to bless an idol in your life. That idol is standing in your way of a right relationship with Him. Your behavior brings out His jealousy.

There will be issues and long-term consequences for your actions. Cracks will form in the foundation of those relationships, and a crack is all the enemy needs. He will pound away at that crack until he bursts the foundation wide open.

Please know that everyone who engages in premarital sex will not be getting a divorce, but will be putting themselves at a greater risk for divorce. There is always a consequence for sin. Focus on the Family quotes several sources on its website that support the fact that premarital sex creates problems in marriage.

2 Corinthians 11:2-3

"For I am jealous for you with godly jealousy. For I have betrothed you to one husband that I may

present you as a chaste virgin to Christ. But I fear,
lest somehow, as the serpent deceived Eve by his
craftiness, so your minds may be corrupted from the
simplicity that is in Christ."

THOUGHT PROVOKING

Why is divorce rampant in our society, especially in the church?

Our spiritual enemy wants to divide and conquer and will stop at nothing to accomplish his goals. We play into his hand when we plug into one another outside the will of God.

When two people marry after having had premarital sex, the percentages are greater that there will be struggles in their marriage than if they had waited to consummate their union. For example, trust can be an issue in the relationship. If they had sex outside of marriage, what makes you think they won't have sex with someone else when married? If they were willing to sleep with you and justify the act, what keeps them from sleeping with another person and justifying the act?

Before entering a physical relationship, you should ask yourself, "Why is he/she so willing to give the gift of their body and soul to me?"

"Women who are sexually active prior to marriage faced considerably higher risk of marital disruption than women who were virgin brides."[4]

"For both genders, we find that virgins have dramatically more stable first marriages..."[5]

"Dissolution rates are substantially higher among those who initiate sexual activity before marriage."[6]

---

4   Joan R. Kahn and Kathryn A. London, "Premarital Sex and the Risk of Divorce," Journal of Marriage and the Family, 53 (1991): 845-855.

5   Edward O. Laumann et al., The Social Organization of Sexuality: Sexual Practices in the United States, (Chicago: University of Chicago Press, 1994), p. 503.

6   Tim B. Heaton, "Factors Contributing to Increasing Marital Stability in the United States," Journal of Family Issues, 23 (2002): 392-409, p. 401, 407.

"Women with more than one intimate relationship prior to marriage have an elevated risk of marital disruption."[7]

"Research shows that adolescent sexuality/premarital sex is associated with marital dissolution."[8]

Many consent to premarital sex for a variety of reasons. Some might say, "It feels good," or "We aren't doing anyone any harm," or "I just wanted her to know how much I loved her." Men often try to convince women that having sex is a way of showing how much they care. If you are a woman ask yourself, "is his reason spiritually healthy or based upon deceptive intent?"

I could have listed additional justifications because they are numerous. Some of you reading this book might even be thinking, "I just like to have sex. After all, God created it and wants us to enjoy His creation." In fact, many who are reading this book will be offended because they have already been justifying their behavior. Please, read the following scripture. Don't you think it is time to rethink your position on abstinence?

1 Corinthians 6:9

"Do you not know that the unrighteous will not inherit the kingdom of God? Do not be deceived. Neither fornicators, nor idolaters, nor adulterers, nor homosexuals, nor sodomites, nor thieves, nor covetous, nor drunkards, nor revilers, nor extortioners will inherit the kingdom of God."

Let's be real with one another. We are all guilty, not just because we fall into one of the categories above. So, don't be too quick to judge

---

7   Jay Teachman, "Premarital Sex, Premarital Cohabitation, and the Risk of Subsequent Marital Dissolution Among Women," Journal of Marriage and Family 65 (2003): 444-455, p. 454.

8   Anthony Paik, "Adolescent Sexuality and Risk of Marital Dissolution," Journal of Marriage and Family 73 (2011): 472-485, p. 483, 484.

others who you think qualify based on the text in the above scripture. We are ALL guilty of sin. The Lord is warning that everyone has sinned and is in need of His saving grace. To be *Born Again* is the only way to enter the kingdom of God.

THOUGHT PROVOKING

Did you know the Lord offers forgiveness whether you are plugged in outside His will or if you refuse to unplug from the world?

He is patient and longs to extend grace to His children. When we finally decide to unplug from the world and plug into Him eternally, He will not only forgive but also grant us grace and mercy. Regardless of the lifestyle we are living or the hardships we encounter, He is always ready to reach out to us and save us.

When we put our trust in Him alone for salvation, He extends His grace and mercy not because we are righteous, but because He is righteous. He washes us clean and empowers us through His Holy Spirit.

Titus 3:4-5

"But when the kindness and the love of God our Savior toward man appeared, not by works of righteousness which we have done, but according to His mercy, He saved us through the washing of regeneration and renewing of the Holy Spirit,"

We must be careful not to use His grace and mercy as an excuse to sin, nor may we justify our sin by stating that God's grace and mercy is sufficient. The challenge scripturally is to live a life that is obedient and respects His grace and mercy. We are all sinners in need of His grace and mercy, no matter how good a life we are living. Thus, it makes sense that we should join Him on our journey.

2 Corinthians 12:9

"And He said to me, 'My grace is sufficient for you, for My strength is made perfect in weakness.' Therefore

most gladly I will rather boast in my infirmities, that
the power of Christ may rest upon me."

You have probably heard the saying, "Mercy is not getting what you deserve, and grace is getting something that you don't deserve." In other words, God extends mercy by forgiving us when we really deserve to be banished from His presence.

Ephesians 2:8

"For by grace you have been saved through faith, and
that not of yourselves; it is the gift of God"

He loves us regardless of our sin. No one is good enough to earn His Love, but His love is available to all.

Romans 3:23

"For all have sinned and fall short of the glory of God

We are then challenged to extend that same grace and mercy to others, even to those who have done us wrong. Unfortunately, our human nature allows us to receive His grace and mercy but doesn't necessarily allow us to extend it to others when their sins have torn us apart. Rather, we ask, "How could God extend grace and mercy to fornicators, idolaters, adulterers, homosexuals, sodomites, thieves, covetous, drunkards, revilers, and extortioners? (From the scripture in 1 Corinthians).

Romans 5:8

"But God demonstrates His own love toward us in
that while we were still sinners, Christ died for us."

The most unfortunate failure we all embrace is blaming God for other people's sins. We should be blaming Satan and the sin he birthed in the garden of Eden. Adam and Eve were disobedient and passed the seed of sin down through natural childbirth. Ever since, when a man and a woman birth a child, Satan's seed of sin is passed on to their sons and daughters by no fault of their own.

Romans 5:12

Therefore, just as through one man sin entered the world, and death through sin, and thus death spread to all men because all have sinned.

Now, we have the Holy Spirit speaking through God's Word so that each of us can understand how to give God our sins and be recipients of His grace and mercy. One would hope that we would make that decision before our sins completely rip apart our lives and the lives of those around us.

We must not forget that just because God is willing to forgive us and extend His grace and mercy doesn't necessarily mean that we are free from the consequences of our sins. Later in the chapter titled, "Unplugging from the World," I relate in more detail my ministry experience inside the Beto I prison. However, I thought it best to share one of those experiences here as an example that while we still reap the consequence of our sinful actions, we can also enjoy the freedom of God's grace and mercy.

One of our team members was walking alongside a prisoner we will call Joe (not his real name) when they passed a baptismal. The prisoner asked, "Mr., what is that?" My team member answered, "Why, Joe, that is where the prison chaplain baptizes anyone who is willing to make a heartfelt decision to trust that God loves them, gave His life for them, and in dying for them, forgave all their sins. Before the chaplain dunks them in the water, they openly make a confession of their devotion to God and Jesus Christ and ask God to come into their heart. Then, they commit to live with Him as their Lord and Savior for the rest of their lives."

Joe responded, "Do you think I could be baptized?"

Our team member asked the chaplain, and Joe was baptized.

Romans 6:23

*"For the wages of sin is death, but the gift of God is
eternal life in Christ Jesus our Lord."*

Sounds like a wonderful story of redemption, wouldn't you agree?
But what if I told you that Joe had murdered a whole family and then set
them on fire. Then, what would your thoughts be?

The fact is that Joe had committed that horrible act and was serv-
ing a life sentence without the chance of parole. His decision for Christ
did not get him out of the physical prison he lives in, but it spiritually
released Joe from Satan's grip on his eternal soul.

Unfortunately, the friends and family members affected by Joe's
sinful act will have to find their own peace with the Lord in order to cope
with their loss and grief. The result of people's sin on others will always
be one of the hardest things to understand and come to grips with.

CHALLENGE QUESTIONS

What are the dangers of entering into a sexual relationship outside of marriage?

What is the main advantage of practicing abstinence in a pre-marital relationship?

What is the true meaning of the statement, "God is a jealous God"?

What idols do you have in your life that might be standing in your way of a right relationship with God?

Do you support the fact that premarital sex creates problems in marriage? If not, what facts do you base your decision on?

What are some ways to extend God's grace and mercy to those who have wronged us?

What are some of the consequences that you have paid as a result of sinful behavior?

How do you deal with the effects of other people's sins?

CHAPTER III

LONG TERM EFFECT OF BEING
UNPLUGGED FROM GOD

*"The man who commits adultery with another man's
wife, he who commits adultery with his neighbor's
wife, the adulterer and the adulteress shall surely be
put to death." (Leviticus 20:10)*

Let me share a real-life story.

A young man took advantage of his future wife by initiating a sexual relationship before they married. He purposed to satisfy his lustful desires not realizing those desires resulted from a God-sized void in his heart. Growing up, his future bride had never received healthy love and affection from her natural father. Unknowingly, she was willing to give herself physically to the young man in hopes of finding true love.

Later, they married, but the marriage was not grounded in Christ. Instead it was based on false feelings for each other. At first, their relationship seemed to be working fine. They enjoyed time with friends and local family members. They were even perceived by others as having a model marriage.

Unknown to the young man, his wife still felt that void for love. She started spending more time with co-workers after work to medicate the inner pain. Her husband was working long hours, and she wasn't about to sit home alone. During that first year, she began sharing her burdens with a male co-worker. After work, he listened to her cries and offered a consoling hug. One hug became two, and before long they engaged in a sexual affair.

The affair became a counterfeit union that gave her a sense of control over her suppressed feelings. However, she didn't consider that she had broken the spiritual covenant of marriage and was no longer providing the intimacy her husband longed for.

In time, the young man learned of the affair and his wife told him that she still loved him. She agreed to break off the relationship with her co-worker, and he made the decision to forgive her. They remained married and sought counseling.

In counseling, neither of them felt comfortable. She couldn't bring herself to be honest, and he didn't understand the God-sized hole in his heart. After a few sessions, they quit counseling and became more active in the church. In doing so, they suppressed their deep-rooted issues. As they continued to immerse themselves in the culture of the church, their marriage seemed to improve. However, they were missing the intimacy that is possible when two people are faithful to one another inside the marriage covenant.

The young man started ushering at church and joined with other men each week to study the bible. His wife began developing deeper relationships within the church. They also had a group of friends that they met with on a regular basis. They participated in a program called, Cursillo, which was a short course in Christianity. This course had a profound impact on the husband. Years later he would learn that his wife had confessed to a Priest attending the closing ceremony that she was actively involved in an affair.

Over the next few years, they had children, and life seemed good. Unfortunately, the church activities and the kids didn't relieve them of the deep-seated root issues within each of their hearts. Not dealing with those issues left an intimacy void, and six years after the first affair, the husband learned that his wife entered into another illicit relationship. This time with a male client she was doing work for.

Still, he was willing to forgive, especially considering their children were young in age. She agreed to go with him to see their priest, and the young man hoped they could find help to save their marriage. However, during one of their counseling sessions with the priest, the young man learned his wife had not ended the first affair right away. When challenged to tell the truth, she went silent, giving the appearance of having no remorse.

She continued the current affair claiming she was in love and rejected all appeals to stay married. The lies and deception had a haunting and humiliating effect. The enemy had used these men to confuse the woman and castigate her husband. She sought a divorce and soon the destruction of the marriage was complete, the family impacted forever.

One of the men she was involved with was attending seminary, was married, and had two children. One must wonder what became of his relationship with his wife. What about his kids? Most of the time, those involved in an illicit affair don't give any thought to the lives they destroy to satisfy their lusts. Devoid of repentance, they are spiritually unplugged and at risk of eternal damnation. Seminary could not protect the man from his sinful nature because his heart was unplugged from the Lord. Neither of the men involved in the affairs ever came forward to ask the betrayed husband for forgiveness.

Hebrews 13:4

"Marriage is honorable among all and the bed undefiled, but fornicators and adulterers God will judge."

Proverbs 6:32-35

"Whoever commits adultery with a woman lacks understanding; He who does so destroys his own soul. Wounds and dishonor he will get, And his reproach will not be wiped away. For jealousy is a husband's fury; Therefore, he will not spare in the day of vengeance. He will accept no recompense, nor will he be appeased though you give many gifts."

Through a lady in church, the young husband was challenged to forgive his former wife, forgive the men who had violated her, and turn over his pain to the Lord. Though difficult, as he made the heart felt decision to plug into God, he began receiving the Lord's healing power.

THOUGHT PROVOKING

Do you believe that forgiveness is not condoning another's actions but releasing the pain from those actions over to God?

God restored a peace to the betrayed husband's heart and healed his pain, but only after he was able to embrace a valuable lesson. God revealed that he was ultimately responsible for his wife's sin, just as Adam had been responsible for Eve's sin. Adam didn't maintain headship in the relationship. The young man was to instruct his wife according to God's command and set the proper example for her.

Had the young man in our story been plugged into God and heeded instruction, he might not have taken advantage of his wife before they married. Had he been a true friend and respected her physically, spiritually, and emotionally, she might have had an opportunity to deal with the pain of her past. She might have been able to plug into God's power source instead of turning to men outside of her marriage. Possibly, he could have saved his family from the hardship of divorce.

The Lord does not give us an out just because we can make a case that we have been violated. (Our own sin must always be dealt with.)

Matthew 5:28

> *"But I say to you that whoever looks at a woman to lust for her has already committed adultery with her in his heart."*

In the Lord's eyes, the young man committed adultery when he violated his future wife before marriage. Plugging in physically before marriage was dangerous because he was relying on the false love of a person rather than on the eternal love of the Father.

Too often, looking at the outward appearance, we think, "Wow, he is good looking, or she is really pretty." What we don't see is what's on the inside. The person might be attractive on the outside but completely damaged on the inside. Sin is enticing and Satan will attempt to lure us into its trap, a trap that has one purpose—eternal destruction.

We have already established that when we seek to fill a void through sexual intercourse before marriage, it is not in God's nature to bless the relationship. God cannot and does not bless sin. He does not tempt us with sin; we are drawn into sin by our own desires that ultimately lead to spiritual death.

James 1:13-15

"Let no one say when he is tempted, "I am tempted by God," for God cannot be tempted by evil, nor does He Himself tempt anyone. But each one is tempted when he is drawn away by his own desires and enticed. Then, when desire has conceived, it gives birth to sin, and sin, when it is full-grown, brings forth death."

No matter what has transpired in your relationships, God can bring good out of any situation. If you find yourself caught in sin's snare, there is but one alternative: unplug from the worldly situation, plug into God, confess your sin, and make amends by asking forgiveness. By plugging into God and keeping your focus on Him, you will protect your heart from the schemes of the enemy.

Proverbs chapter seven relates a story that is extremely relevant for our purposes. Considering the length of the passage I have broken down the key points and encourage you to take the time to read the passage in its entirety.

"My son, keep my words, And treasure my commands within you...Say to wisdom, "You are my sister," and call understanding your nearest kin, That they may keep you from the immoral woman, from the seductress who flatters with her words...I perceived among the youths a young man devoid of understanding, and passing along the street near her corner, he took the path to her house...In the black and dark night, there a woman met him, with the attire of a harlot and a crafty heart. She was loud and rebellious...With her enticing speech, she caused him to yield...she seduced him. Immediately, he went after her, as an ox goes to the slaughter or as a fool to the correction of the stocks...Now, therefore,

listen to me, my children; pay attention to the words of my mouth. Do not let your hearts turn aside to her ways...And all who were slain by her were strong men. Her house is the way to hell..."

Notice the last two sentences: "And all who were slain by her were strong men. Her house is the way to hell." The seductress in this story is not just a man or a woman, it is a spiritual enemy—sin residing in the heart and its desire is to destroy all that are tempted.

Genesis 4:7

"If you do well, will you not be accepted? And if you do not do well, sin lies at the door. And its desire is for you, but you should rule over it."

If you are in the wrong kind of relationship, and by wrong, I mean any relationship in which you have entered an intimate physical relationship or in which you are spiritually and emotionally attached outside of God's will, then it makes sense, in light of what the Lord wants for you, to unplug or separate from the world. You must rule over the sinful nature, it is not too late.

There is no easy way to say it, if you don't make this separation, you are going to have problems. Life is already hard enough without inviting a direct attack from the enemy. Satan sets a trap by appealing to our ignorance, using our insecurities, and appealing to the gaping hole in our hearts. The hole in our hearts can be filled only with Jesus Christ the Lord. He is the only one who brings true fulfillment—eternal fulfillment.

CHALLENGE QUESTIONS

Have you ever had a God-sized void in your heart?

What is broken when a spouse has an affair with someone outside of the marriage?

Do perpetrators give any thought to the lives they destroy as they satisfy their lusts?

What does forgiveness bring?

Why was Adam responsible for Eve's sin?

How does sin lead to spiritual death?

CHAPTER IV

UNPLUGGING FROM THE WORLD

"That we should no longer be children, tossed to and fro and carried about with every wind of doctrine by the trickery of men, in the cunning craftiness of deceitful plotting, but, speaking the truth in love, may grow up in all things into Him who is the head— Christ." (Ephesians 4:14-15)

We will never be able to plug fully into God's power strip until we are willing to unplug from the world. We must unplug from the world to protect our hearts from being carried away by various doctrines taught by men similar to the priest from chapter one. We must unplug from the lies bombarding us daily. Many people are following the doctrines of individuals who are wretched sinners just like us. Thus, out of our ignorance and longing for answers, we have allowed ourselves to be "tossed to and fro and carried about with every wind of doctrine."

Scripture educates us in the proper way of thinking and assists us in keeping the proper perspective in life. Many doctrines we hear today are products of cunning, crafty, and deceitful men. What makes us think the doctrine of a sinner is loftier than the doctrine presented in God's Word?

We have bought into sin's deceptive nature for a long time, and as a result, our hearts have become tethered to the lying nature of those doctrines. There is only one true doctrine—Holy Scripture—given to us by inspiration of God. In the scripture below, Timothy does not say SOME scripture, but ALL scripture is profitable.

2 Timothy 3:16

> *"All Scripture is given by inspiration of God, and is profitable for doctrine, for reproof, for correction, for instruction in righteousness,"*

Most of us are content living the way we always have. Especially those of us who are financially stable. We give into sin, not realizing that a day will come that we will ultimately pay the consequences for our sins. Unfortunately, for that day to be realized, it usually takes something or someone hitting us upside the head before we are ready to listen. When that day comes, the consequence will be much harder to bear.

You have probably seen the cartoon of the man struggling with a decision. He has an angel sitting on one shoulder suggesting the right course of action and the devil sitting on the other shoulder suggesting the wrong course of action. The man turns his head to the right and then to the left, and the debate roars on between the forces of good and evil. Finally, reaching a decision, he gives into temptation and chooses the wrong course of action. The devil stands tall, snickering in victory, assuming he has won the battle for the man's heart.

I relate this cartoon because we have all been that person. Faced with decisions in life, we make the choice to follow the devil's suggested course of action. On the surface, the devil's option might have seemed more exciting and adventurous than the angel's option. Inevitably, when we choose the devil's path, we pay a consequence for our action. The consequences continue for a long time and may cause a tremendous amount of pain.

Why do we not heed God's voice in the first place? Why are we not obedient to His Word? Why do we punish ourselves and those around us by allowing "the evil one" access to our hearts?

THOUGHT PROVOKING

Do you agree it would be wise to train ourselves to unplug from the voice of sin and plug into God's voice?

2 Corinthians 10:4-5

"For the weapons of our warfare are not carnal but mighty in God for pulling down strongholds, casting down arguments and every high thing that exalts itself against the knowledge of God, bringing every thought into captivity to the obedience of Christ."

The Bible is the living Word of God and instructs us how to live our lives. Through the Word, the Holy Spirit comes alive in our heart. The Holy Spirit's voice gives us access to our Father in Heaven. His is a voice of love, a voice of wisdom, a voice of peace, and a voice of hope.

James 1:19-25

"So then, my beloved brethren, let every man be swift to hear, slow to speak, slow to wrath, for the wrath of man does not produce the righteousness of God. Therefore, lay aside all filthiness and overflow of wickedness and receive with meekness the implanted word, which is able to save your souls. But be doers of the word and not hearers only, deceiving yourselves. For if anyone is a hearer of the word and not a doer, he is like a man observing his natural face in a mirror, for he observes himself, goes away, and immediately forgets what kind of man he was. But he who looks into the perfect law of liberty and continues in it and is not a forgetful hearer but a doer of the work, this one will be blessed in what he does."

Each person should ask, "Do I know His voice when I hear it?" In the previous verse, we are instructed to be swift to hear, slow to speak, and slow to wrath. We are then instructed to be doers of the Word. Hearing the Word is easy; obeying is more difficult. However, it is in obeying the Word that we begin to know His voice.

The man with the angel on one shoulder and the devil on the other was listening, but he did not obey. When we obey, God's Holy

Spirit comes alive within us; His word comes alive within us. We then long to obey.

Luke 6:46-49

"But why do you call Me 'Lord, Lord,' and not do the things which I say? Whoever comes to Me, and hears My sayings and does them, I will show you whom he is like. He is like a man building a house, who dug deep and laid the foundation on the rock. And when the flood arose, the stream beat vehemently against that house, and could not shake it, for it was founded on the rock. But he who heard and did nothing is like a man who built a house on the earth without a foundation, against which the stream beat vehemently; and immediately it fell. And the ruin of that house was great."

In the Old Testament, God guided Abraham, Isaac, and Jacob laying the foundation for His people and in the New Testament He blazed the trail for us by becoming human and experiencing our pain. He knows the plan for our lives. Patience is the key to obedience, and we are to avoid plugging into the world no matter how enticing sin may appear.

As we embrace the Word, we begin to trust that God knows what is best and is preparing our path in life. It helps us build a spiritual foundation on the rock of Christ, a rock that cannot and will not be moved by the storms of life. He longs to have fellowship with us and promises that if we seek Him, we will find Him.

Deuteronomy 4:29

"But from there you will seek the LORD your God, and you will find Him if you seek Him with all your heart and with all your soul."

God's voice is longing to be heard, longing to be heeded, and longing to direct us in righteousness. However, God is respectful of our will and does not force His agenda on us. God's voice is "still" and "small" and desires to penetrate the inner depths of our soul. In the following verse God brings revelation to Elijah.

1 Kings 19:11-12

> *"Then, He said, 'Go out and stand on the mountain before the LORD.' And behold, the LORD passed by, and a great and strong wind tore into the mountains and broke the rocks in pieces before the LORD, but the LORD was not in the wind; and after the wind an earthquake, but the LORD was not in the earthquake; and after the earthquake a fire, but the LORD was not in the fire; and after the fire a still small voice."*

THOUGHT PROVOKING

During your most difficult times, have you ever felt God appeared to be deaf?

Has there been a time in your life when you were hurting so badly that you wanted God to scream out leaving no doubt He was listening? Or has there been a time when you were the one screaming in hopes God would say something just to let you know He was listening?

These thoughts can lure us into sin's trap. Groping for answers, we become vulnerable to the possibility of hearing the wrong voice. If we are in turmoil and our inner voice is screaming, we will be unsettled. Similarly, if we are screaming out loud, we will not be able to hear God speaking, thereby putting ourselves further at risk. The Lord gives us instructions 24/7, but oftentimes we choose not to hear him or allow life's struggles to render us deaf.

Think back on a time when a child has screamed at you. What was your reaction? Did you scream back, or did you lower your voice? When we lower our voice, children will eventually stop screaming so they can hear what we are saying. In fact, the lower our voice becomes, the more attentive they become.

Why does this technique work with children? Could it be that inherent within all of us is a longing to hear the voice of reason? A voice that is peaceful, loving, and wise. Why not try this technique next time a child, friend, co-worker, or anyone raises their voice toward you? Speak softly and lower your tone. See if they cease their outburst and strain to hear what you are saying.

When someone is out of control, and if we will remain calm, the other person will eventually become played out and cease talking. Only then is it possible to have a civil conversation. Thus, it is only when we are settled in our spirit that we hear the "still small voice" of our Father in Heaven and can have a civil conversation with Him. When we cease our striving, sit still, and listen, we come to the realization that His voice of power has been there all along. He is always there, speaking to us even amid our turmoil and the whirlwind of life's circumstances.

Growing up, I was the youngest of three boys, each three and one-half years apart, and we fought constantly. As the youngest, you can imagine the outcome of our skirmishes. When my brothers gained the upper hand, I would scream bloody murder to draw attention to my predicament. I wanted their sin exposed–I wanted them to pay.

When our father arrived on the scene, he would become frustrated with my screaming. His first response was to encourage me to stand up and defend myself. Of course, when I did not calm down, I was punished, thus intensifying my pain. I remember thinking, "How unfair. After all, they are the ones to blame." I gave no thought to what part I played to invite the punishment.

During my screams for attention, I was not able to hear my father's instruction; therefore, the covering I desired, right or wrong, was seemingly unavailable. His was the voice of wisdom, instruction, and sound reasoning. He was encouraging me to stand strong so not be controlled by others, but I did not hear him. I was so consumed with screaming that I missed out on his instruction.

Anger and unforgiveness blinds us and, at times, results in our yelling or screaming. Some of you reading these words may be thinking, "I don't yell or scream. I just go silent." I assure you silence can be just as damaging or more so. Silence is often a passive-aggressive way of expressing anger and frustration. Some might even embrace the attitude, "I don't get mad; I get even!"

We might be hiding behind a wall of silence to suppress our fear and pain, thereby shutting out any voice that would force us to deal with that fear and pain. Anyone getting too close to our issues becomes a threat and eventually the object of our transference, which is the redirection of feelings and desires.

When we transfer our fear, pain, or circumstances onto other people, we keep the attention turned away from us, and in so doing, we avoid dealing with the issue. In the context of personal and social circles, transference can be described as a pathological issue. When people meet a new person, who reminds them of someone else, they unconsciously infer that the new person has traits similar to the person previously known.[9] Future relationships are in jeopardy because we choose people dealing with the same damaging issues we are.

THOUGHT PROVOKING

Have you ever been faced with a relationship that reminded you of a previous damaged relationship? Did you wonder how you made the wrong choice?

Many of us fall into one of two categories at some point in our lives: overt screamers or covert screamers. The inner desire either longs to resolve the problem or ignore the problem. Either way, if we are unstable spiritually, the problem will never be completely resolved. Situation or circumstance may change and, in some cases, even get better, nevertheless, it will just be a matter of time until a new conflict arises.

You can change the names and the events, but the emotions and the patterns remain the same. Evil's desire is for us to either scream out or suppress the anger and frustration and ultimately win the victory over our hearts.

Several years ago, a good friend who was smart, bold, and, by the world's standards, successful was faced with a dilemma. The very traits that helped him be successful became barriers to his effectiveness as a manager. When he did not get his way, he raged outwardly at the people working for him and overpowered them. Over time, those same people began to avoid him so not to excite his wrath.

---

9   Andersen, S. M. & Berk., M. (1998). The social-cognitive model of transference: Experiencing past relationships in the present. Current Directions in Psychological Science, 7(4), 109-115.

Eventually, word about his behavior spread, and his reputation in the community suffered. His approach was not well received. He was able to overpower weaker people, but not those who were stronger and more secure. Some even resisted out of spite and exercised their own form of dominance. Many would not do business with him. Like so many of us, he was suffering from the events of his past, and his behavior was destroying everything he had worked so hard to build.

Personally, I encountered a similar experience that exposed an area within my own heart. Two friends called saying they wanted to meet one Sunday afternoon. I soon learned they had a preconceived agenda. They were concerned about my behavior in certain situations. As they voiced their concern, God exposed an area of unforgiveness I had been holding on to. I was tethered to a wrongful act perpetrated against me. I resisted their counsel at first, but they were not to be denied, so I began to listen attentively.

As I calmed, I began to hear the Lord's voice of reason emanate from my friends. They cared enough to tell me the truth and were willing to stand toe to toe with me and persevere long enough for me to hear what God was speaking through them. I started thanking God for their friendship.

When we don't heed our Father's instruction and obey His commands, our behavior forms a destructive pattern and damages relationships; insecurity and immaturity often develop. Previous wrongs or abuse may have been unfair, but they keep us bound. At times, we might even feel frustrated and trapped. Quite possibly a similar frustration and despair was felt as a child, only we might not associate the feeling with our childhood.

By not letting go of our issues, we ignorantly allow them to maintain a hold on us and negatively impact our lives. Not dealing with these issues and our resulting patterns can and will stand in the way of future success.

THOUGHT PROVOKING

Why do we wait until our life is completely upside down before we begin crying out to God?

Usually, we do not cry out for help until our lives are completely upside down. We finally get to the point where we are willing to lay our issues at God's throne of grace and let Him take on our burdens.

Hebrews 4:16

"Let us therefore come boldly to the throne of grace, that we may obtain mercy and find grace to help in time of need."

When we open our hearts we will find His grace, receive His mercy, and be able to hear His voice. Only then do we discover that God has been there all along and He is not out to punish us, but to provide us a *future and a hope.*

Jeremiah 29:11-13

"For I know the thoughts that I think toward you, says the LORD, thoughts of peace and not of evil, to give you a future and a hope. Then you will call upon Me and go and pray to Me, and I will listen to you. And you will seek Me and find Me when you search for Me with all your heart."

God longs to be in relationship with us and help us uncover the lies that have been holding us back from receiving His power. In the following scripture from the book of John, Jesus is speaking to his disciples, offering His farewell speech. He is giving them insight that the helper, the Holy Spirit of God, will come after His death to be their voice of reason and provide instruction on how to live their lives.

John 16:5-7

"But now I go away to Him who sent Me, and none of you asks Me, 'Where are You going?' But because I have said these things to you, sorrow has filled your heart. Nevertheless, I tell you the truth. It is to your advantage that I go away; for if I do not go away, the Helper will not come to you."

We are not much different from the people in Jesus' day. After His death, many did not embrace His eternal truths. In fact, like many of us today, they attempted to control life by holding on to destructive patterns of behavior. They did not acknowledge the inner voice of the Holy Spirit, telling them there was a better way. They ignored the voice of reason instructing them to act or react contrary to their flesh.

THOUGHT PROVOKING

Have you ever ignored the voice of reason?

From childhood, we begin to form behaviors to avoid pain. Those behaviors become so ingrained into our inner core that they seem necessary for us to maintain our existence. The behaviors become walls behind which we live. Those walls keep out anyone and anything that would have us address the pain and the fear associated with that pain. The walls of behavior become a part of who we are.

Only through revelation can we get to the point where we will acknowledge our walls. At that point, we admit something is wrong and that we must change. Oftentimes, we cry out in pain and are not even aware of whom we are crying out to. The voice of reason responds, but instead of listening to the positive inner voice whispering in our ears, we listen to the inner voice that is screaming at us. Some people turn to alcohol, drugs, food, or some other substance to medicate the pain—to silence the voice.

Some might appear together on the outside, but they are a mess on the inside. They have bought into the lie that they have found a work-able solution. They believe the walls surrounding them have provided a crutch that will allow them to function without going completely crazy. Those crutches offer false support, eventually driving us deeper into denial. As with any crutch, there comes a time that you must put down the crutch in order to stand on your own two feet.

Early in the book we established that God understands all, sees all, and is a loving God. He helps us identify the areas where we have been damaged and through brokenness longs to take our fears and pains upon Himself. His desire is to remove permanently the damage from our hearts. We must unplug from the world, our past heartaches, and painful experiences and plug into a loving God.

In Chapter three, I mentioned a ministry that I had the tremendous opportunity to serve with at Beto I, a maximum-security prison in Palestine, Texas. Our team had spent several weeks in preparation for our time at the prison. Upon our arrival, we were ushered through a door into a large open room with chairs arranged in a circle. Each of us took a seat leaving a seat on each side of us for the inmates. Soon, another door opened, and in came the inmates. The guards instructed them to take a seat, and slowly they became dispersed among us. Next, we passed a microphone and asked everyone to state their name and where they were from.

The prison chaplain had invited the toughest men, those considered the leaders among the various groups within the prison population. The only reason they agreed to attend was the chaplain's offer of a weekend off from work and unlimited cookies. Normally, they would have chosen not to be in the same room with each other. It was the chaplain's hope that if these men would unplug from the world and plug into God, they could lead other men to plug into God.

Prior to the event, people associated with the ministry from around the world, wrote letters of encouragement to the inmates by name who would be attending. Over the course of the weekend, each of our team members also wrote letters and we separated them into individual sacks, one for each inmate.

On the final day, we gave each of them a sack filled with their letters. Many of the inmates had never received a letter from the outside. As they received their sack full of sealed letters, there was much excitement. It is important to note that they had never been allowed to unseal a letter; all correspondence from the outside world was prescreened. So, as they opened and read those letters, tears began to flow. Eventually, there was not one dry eye in the room. Now mind you, crying in prison is a sign of weakness, and these were the toughest men in the joint.

What these men experienced was brokenness, and that brokenness gave them access to be plugged into other Christian believers through the power of the Holy Spirit. At the end of our time together, we offered each of them individually an opportunity to believe in and put their trust in Jesus Christ for eternal salvation. Many of the men made a heartfelt decision that day to unplug from their worldly past and to plug into God for all eternity. Obviously, none of them were allowed to leave prison, but they were allowed to escape the pain associated with the reason they were incarcerated. The weekend was a monumental experience, one they will draw on for a lifetime—for all eternity.

The following is a short test to determine if you have ever been grounded in the lies of our spiritual enemy. Answer True or False if you have ever heard any of the following voices.

GROUNDED IN LIES SELF-TEST

T / F   You are all alone.

T / F   You are worthless.

T / F   No one else has your thoughts.

T / F   No one wants to hear your story.

T / F   No one cares about you.

T / F   If you were really a Christian, you would be stronger.

T / F   If you were really a Christian, you would not do the things you do.

T / F   If you were really a Christian, you wouldn't have those thoughts.

T / F   God loves everyone else, but he doesn't love you.

THOUGHT PROVOKING

If you answered true to any of these lies, do you think you are unplugged from God or maybe your plug is loose?

At some point, everyone experiences negative thoughts. We might even believe the lie from the spiritual enemy of our flesh that God has abandoned or given up on us. Satan wants us to feel condemned, guilty, and ashamed. He infiltrates our minds through our sinful nature and has us believe we are more deserving of death than life. He bases his argument on the facts of our past bad decisions and destructive behaviors, which should give us even more reason to make the decision to unplug from the world.

Hebrews 13:5

"...For He Himself has said, 'I will never leave you nor forsake you.'"

God will never abandon His children. His grace and mercy are powerful in breaking the strongholds the world has placed on each of us. Ask yourself, "Have I unplugged from my past? From the world? Am I plugged into God and His eternal power source?

CHALLENGE QUESTIONS

What are some of the false doctrines being taught by man?

Can you think of a time when you heeded the voice of the devil and not the angel on your shoulder?

What was the outcome?

What do we gain by reading the Word of God?

What are the benefits of obeying God's Word?

Why does God speak to us in a still small voice?

Have you ever felt during the toughest times of your life that God is deaf?

What are some of the crutches we use to medicate our emotional pain?

How do we unplug from the world?

CHAPTER V

❦

ETERNALLY PLUGGING INTO GOD

"Seeing then that we have a great High Priest who has passed through the heavens, Jesus the Son of God, let us hold fast our confession. For we do not have a High Priest who cannot sympathize with our weaknesses, but was in all points tempted as we are, yet without sin."
(Hebrews 4:14-15)

The spirit flows through us into our hearts when we truly believe in Christ' death and resurrection and trust Him alone for our salvation. By trusting in Jesus Christ, embracing His death as a blood sacrifice for our sins, and acknowledging that His resurrection and ascension has given us access to God the Father. At that very moment, the Holy Spirit enters our heart, we are instantly and eternally plugged into God— the Ultimate Power Source.

Jesus was God incarnate and, as a result, had God's nature inherent within him in human form. He was fully human and fully God. God's power source was deeply imbedded in his heart. In essence, you could say that Jesus was *Plugged In* and, thus able to walk through life enduring every temptation known to man, "Yet without sin," as we read in the opening verse.

Pause for a moment and think of the rejection Christ endured. He was falsely accused, spat on, and beaten to the point of non-recognition. He was forced to carry the tree He would be nailed to. He paid the ultimate price: death on the cross. That tree would play a role in the preparation of our eternal freedom; therefore, it makes sense to follow His example and walk in His ways, fully embracing His word.

In the scripture John 3: 5-6 Jesus is instructing Nicodemus, "Most assuredly, I say to you, unless one is born of water and the Spirit, he cannot enter the kingdom of God. That which is born of the flesh is flesh, and that which is born of the Spirit is spirit."

Let us focus closely on Jesus' statement, "Unless one is born of water and the Spirit, he cannot enter the kingdom of God."

THOUGHT PROVOKING

What do you think Jesus meant by the above statement?

When the baby is in the mother's womb, it is immersed in amniotic fluid, and not until the baby emerges from the womb is the umbilical cord cut. The baby then begins to breathe on its own and is cleansed of the waxy substance, vernix, which has covered the body.

Speaking to Nicodemus, Jesus was using the words "water and the Spirit," to help him grasp fully what He meant by a new birth. Jesus' words are just as profound today. His desire is for us to go deeper in our revelatory understanding of His Word. When we trust in Christ and become *Born Again,* we are cut away from the world and renewed spiritually. Cleansed from sin, we begin to breathe anew. Unfortunately, we remain in this world until we enter Heaven and we will face challenges as a result of our new birth.

John 17:14

> "I have given them Your word; and the world has hated them because they are not of the world, just as I am not of the world."

After reading the above scripture, it would be wise for us to explore Christs' words, "born of water and the Spirit," on a deeper level. Most theologians will correctly tell you that neither is a necessary requirement for salvation. However, I want to challenge you that they are an integral part of plugging into God's power strip and grasping fully the power of the eternal life Jesus was expressing to Nicodemus, *The Kingdom of God.*

WATER BAPTISM

Plugging into God through water baptism is an outward expression of your faith based on an inward decision.

1 Peter 3:18-22

"For Christ also suffered once for sins, the just for the unjust, that He might bring us to God, being put to death in the flesh but made alive by the Spirit, by whom also He went and preached to the spirits in prison, who formerly were disobedient, when once the Divine longsuffering waited in the days of Noah, while the ark was being prepared, in which a few, that is, eight souls, were saved through water. There is also an antitype which now saves us—baptism (not the removal of the filth of the flesh, but the answer of a good conscience toward God), through the resurrection of Jesus Christ, who has gone into heaven and is at the right hand of God, angels and authorities and powers having been made subject to Him."

Many will tell you that if you were baptized as a baby or a young child you have no need to be baptized again. Personally, growing up in the Methodist church, I was "sprinkled" as an infant, and I am thankful to my parents for walking me down the aisle and handing me to the minister that day. People need as much covering in this world as they can get. That act serves to remind the parent and parishioners that they have a part to play and a responsibility in raising the child according to the Holy Scriptures. One would hope that they would take that duty seriously.

Some Christians today will argue that people need to wait and be baptized when they reach an age where they can make their own personal profession of faith. How can you argue against that point? After all, God wants us to make a free will choice, and folks can do that only when they are old enough to understand what that choice represents.

Given the fact that there is a battle for our souls, hopefully we can all agree that some form of baptism should be important and necessary in the life of a believer. It is not my desire to argue or theologically debate the act of baptism, especially since various denominations have differing opinions about baptism.

However, I strongly believe that the decision to be baptized is one that all believers should consider based on Christ's own example. Jesus' decision to be baptized by John makes a clear statement that baptism is a necessary aspect of plugging into God's power. Jesus entered the water of baptism and emerged ready to redeem us from our sins and allow the promises of God to be passed on to us.

These were the promises given to Abraham. All believers are children of Abraham and can claim His promises through Jesus' redeeming sacrifice—the promises of the Spirit through faith.

Galatians 3:13-14

"Christ has redeemed us from the curse of the law, having become a curse for us (for it is written, "Cursed is everyone who hangs on a tree"), that the blessing of Abraham might come upon the Gentiles in Christ Jesus, that we might receive the promise of the Spirit through faith."

John the Baptist was Jesus' cousin, and he awaited the day of the coming of the Lord and devoted his life to telling people about the Lord through water baptism. He was not adorned with fine linen, and he did not live in a palace. Instead, he wore camel hair, ate locusts, and lived out among nature. John had one purpose in life, and he did not deviate from that purpose.

John 1:23

"He said: 'I am The voice of one crying in the wilderness: 'Make straight the way of the LORD,' 'as the prophet Isaiah said.'"

In the next scripture, we see that Jesus came to John to be baptized. John had a tough time reconciling the fact that Jesus had come to him to be baptized. Jesus shows up in a humble manner holding himself to the same standard He requires of us—Jesus came to set the standard for everyone. This passage leads us to believe that Jesus was not just sprinkled, but immersed.

Matthew 3:13-17

"Then Jesus came from Galilee to John at the Jordan to be baptized by him. And John tried to prevent Him, saying, 'I need to be baptized by You, and are You coming to me?' But Jesus answered and said to him, 'Permit it to be so now, for thus it is fitting for us to fulfill all righteousness' Then he allowed Him. When He had been baptized, Jesus came up immediately from the water, and behold, the heavens were opened to Him, and He saw the Spirit of God descending like a dove and alighting upon Him. And suddenly a voice came from heaven, saying, 'This is My beloved Son in whom I am well pleased.'"

The Greek word for baptism used here is bap-tid'-zo: to make whelmed (i.e. fully wet)[10]

In the waters of baptism, the Spirit washes away our sin, and from that day forward, other people should see a definite change in our spiritual appearance, change enacted by the Spirit's transforming power working in our lives.

In the case of our Savior Jesus, He came up out of the waters of baptism, and God affirmed Him, proclaiming, "This is My beloved Son, in whom I am well pleased." There is no greater authority, wouldn't you agree?

I don't know about you, but if I were standing on the banks of the Jordan that day, I would have scrambled to be the first in line to be baptized. I would not be debating whether I should be sprinkled or dunked.

---

10   Strong, James. 1894. Dictionary of the words in The Greek Testament. New York: Hunt & Eaton.

I would want all God had for me. Furthermore, any argument about the timing of baptism would be silenced at that moment.

Based on this scripture in Matthew, there are two points worth emphasizing:

1. John did not understand that Jesus needed to be baptized. Instead, John attempted to prevent it by saying, "I need to be baptized by You, and are You coming to me?"

So often, scripture can be confusing because it speaks to us on a level that is hard to visualize in the physical realm. Here, in this passage, we see that even John the Baptist, who obviously understood who Jesus was, became confused when faced with the prospect of baptizing Jesus. Today, are we much different from John or Nicodemus? Even though we do not understand on an intellectual level, we can believe on a spiritual level that Christ knows what He is doing.

2. Jesus did not rebuke John, but calmly responded by saying, "Permit it to be so now, for thus it is fitting for us to fulfill all righteousness."

Jesus understood the importance of making a public profession of His own faith and commitment to His Father. He was spiritually washed in righteousness and ready to begin His ministry, ready to establish His dominion and sovereignty over a fallen world. Jesus entered the waters of baptism representing sinful man and emerged in the spiritual sense, *Born Again*, cleansed from all unrighteousness. Like the baby emerging from the womb and being cleansed, He was cleansed in righteousness.

> *The word for righteousness used here is the Greek word dikaiosune from dikaios meaning innocent, holy: just, meet, right.*[11]

Jesus made a public display of His eternal commitment, and God the Father affirmed Him. John and everyone else present that day were eyewitnesses to this paramount event.

---

11   Strong, James. 1894. Dictionary of the words in The Greek Testament. New York: Hunt & Eaton.

Matthew 3:16

"When He had been baptized, Jesus came up immediately from the water; and behold, the heavens were opened to Him, and He saw the Spirit of God descending like a dove and alighting upon Him."

Therefore, it would make sense to conclude that the only prerequisite for baptism is the belief that Christ shed His blood for your sins, conquered death, and was resurrected to new life with God the Father. Your challenge and my challenge are in placing our trust in Him alone for salvation.

BAPTISM OF THE HOLY SPIRIT

In the verses below we learn that when we become baptized with the Holy Spirit, we are "endued with power on high," and we are given a "Helper," who empowers us and will abide with us forever.

John 14:15-17

"'If you love Me, keep My commandments. And I will pray the Father, and He will give you another Helper, that He may abide with you forever—the Spirit of truth, whom the world cannot receive because it neither sees Him nor knows Him; but you know Him, for He dwells with you and will be in you.'"

Luke 24:49

"'Behold, I send the Promise of My Father upon you; but tarry in the city of Jerusalem until you are endued with power from on high.'"

In this passage from Luke, Jesus was speaking to the disciples after being raised from the dead. They had no idea what He meant by his statements. However, when confronted with the resurrected Savior, they were obedient and followed His instruction.

THOUGHT PROVOKING

Don't you want all that the God of the universe has for you?

I think you will agree that if you and I were among those present that day, having been witnesses to His crucifixion and His resurrection, we would have been obedient as well. Jesus says that the spirit "will be in you," which leads no doubt that after being *Born Again* we receive the spirit within us. After we make a heartfelt decision and put our trust in Jesus Christ, he sends the "Spirit of Truth," which we learn in the scripture below is the Holy Spirit.

John 20:21-22

"So Jesus said to them again, "Peace to you! As the Father has sent Me, I also send you." And when He had said this, He breathed on them, and said to them, "Receive the Holy Spirit."

The prophetic word of John the Baptist became a reality. John had received God's instruction that Jesus would come baptizing with the Holy Spirit. His instruction came from no greater authority.

John 1:33

"I did not know Him, but He who sent me to baptize with water said to me, 'Upon whom you see the Spirit descending, and remaining on Him, this is He who baptizes with the Holy Spirit.'"

We should be safe in assuming that the men and women who were present that day had already been immersed in the waters of baptism.

However, in the book of Acts, we learn that many of Jesus' disciples, living at the same time as Paul, did not even know a Holy Spirit existed. They obviously had accepted conceptually that Christ was the Savior, but by their own admission, had only been baptized according to John, meaning they had been baptized in water only. God obviously had something greater in mind for them.

Acts 19:1-7

"And it happened, while Apollos was at Corinth, that Paul, having passed through the upper regions, came to Ephesus. And finding some disciples, he said to them, 'Did you receive the Holy Spirit when you believed?' So they said to him, 'We have not so much as heard whether there is a Holy Spirit.' And he said to them, 'Into what then were you baptized?' So they said, 'Into John's baptism.' Then Paul said, 'John indeed baptized with a baptism of repentance, saying to the people that they should believe on Him who would come after him, that is, on Christ Jesus.' When they heard this, they were baptized in the name of the Lord Jesus. And when Paul had laid hands on them, the Holy Spirit came upon them, and they spoke with tongues and prophesied. Now the men were about twelve in all."

This was not Jesus laying hands on them, but another Christian laying hands on them and as a result, the "Holy Spirit came upon them." When Paul laid hands on them, they were more firmly plugged into God's power strip than they had been with just the water baptism. There should be no reason for modern day Christians to debate the need for or importance of being baptized with the Holy Spirit.

BAPTISM WITH FIRE

In Matthew, we learn Jesus will not only come baptizing with the Holy Spirit, but with fire. There are many debates about this scripture, specifically in reference to fire.

Matthew 3:11

> *"I indeed baptize you with water unto repentance, but He who is coming after me is mightier than I, whose sandals I am not worthy to carry. He will baptize you with the Holy Spirit and fire."*

We need to be careful when reading the word, for like Nicodemus, we tend to define Christ's words in a physical sense based on our intellectual understanding. Many Bible scholars have debated exactly what John the Baptist was saying. If you would like to read more accounts about the baptism of the Holy Spirit, you can do so in the book of Acts. Two accounts can be found in Acts 2:1-4 and Acts 8:12-17.

We know that baptism with fire is not fire in the literal sense. However, we could rightly assume the fire is from above and is God's impartation of His Holy Spirit. We learn in Hebrews that God is a consuming fire.

Hebrews 12:28-29

> *"Therefore, since we are receiving a kingdom which cannot be shaken, let us have grace, by which we may serve God acceptably with reverence and godly fear. For our God is a consuming fire."*

THOUGHT PROVOKING

Is it the fire that produces tongues as in the previous scripture we read in Acts, or is the fire meant to be the pending judgment of non-Christians? Then again, could it be some supernatural baptism that we really do not know much about?

The Holy Spirit comes and brings conviction to the hearts of sinners who have truly trusted in Jesus as their Lord and Savior. His is a cleansing and purifying fire for the born-again believer at a level not previously encountered.

Malachi 3:1-3

> *"Behold, I send My messenger, and he will prepare the way before Me. And the Lord, whom you seek, will suddenly come to His temple, even the Messenger of the covenant, in whom you delight. Behold, He is coming' says the LORD of hosts. 'But who can endure the day of His coming? And who can stand when He appears? For He is like a refiner's fire and like launderers' soap. He will sit as a refiner and a purifier of silver; He will purify the sons of Levi and purge them as gold and silver that they may offer to the LORD an offering in righteousness.'"*

There have been so many intellectual debates over the subject of fire that we could very easily be confused. The main thing to keep in mind is this: He gives His spirit completely and fully to all who are willing to trust in Him by faith, believing in their hearts His sacrifice for their sins through His death and resurrection. However, as with anything in life, we grow, mature, and gain new and fresh revelations at various times.

The canon of scripture has been closed, which means there will be no new revelation from man. The only true revelation is already written and is contained in the scriptures. The Lord will continue to reveal himself in a fresh way through His Word as we are able to receive it by faith.

The fire that the Lord will bring into the life of believers is one that cleanses them from their sinful natures. The fire the Lord will bring into the life of non-believers will be a consuming fire that in the end bears witness of their sins and bring judgment that will separate them from the Father for all eternity.

Isaiah 5:24

> *"Therefore, as the fire devours the stubble, and the flame consumes the chaff, so their root will be as*

rottenness, and their blossom will ascend like dust because they have rejected the law of the LORD of hosts and despised the word of the Holy One of Israel."

Revelation 20:15

"And anyone not found written in the Book of Life was cast into the lake of fire."

How can we put Jesus in a box and limit the scope of His Ministry? If you have not already, I would encourage you to let go of your inherent nature to doubt, open your heart, and put your trust in Him. He wants the best for you.

I once heard how a sword was made. The master craftsman would thrust the blade into the fire, hold it up to the light, check for impurities, and then pound them out of the blade. He continued this process, until finally the blade was thrust in the fire one last time. The craftsman then pulled it from the fire and etched his signature onto the blade. His signature was assurance that the blade would not fail in battle.

I can say with confidence that I have been through the refiner's fire. My life continues to have the flaws hammered out of it, and the difference in my life today is evident to all who know me. Each day I ask God to search my heart, and to purify me, for I want to be prepared each time I am given an opportunity to speak the truth into the lives of others.

THOUGHT PROVOKING

What would happen if you asked the Lord to baptize you with the Holy Spirit and fire? Shouldn't we desire to be "endued with power from on high"?

In John 3:8 Jesus spoke of receiving this power when He said, "The wind blows where it wishes, and you hear the sound of it, but cannot tell where it comes from and where it goes. So it is with everyone born of the Spirit." If we could see the Spirit working, we would not be able to handle the power associated with it. The Spirit is working everywhere, and when we become *Born Again*, we just start to tap into God's power strip.

A good friend of mine is blind; however, she can see more clearly than anyone I know. All her senses are alive; she has trained herself to utilize all the senses God has given her. For that reason, she sees in the Spirit because that is the only eyesight she has. She might be physically blind, but she has tapped into God's power strip, and that power guides, protects, and empowers her every day.

We need to be veiled in the Holy Spirit to overcome life's worries, which are trivial compared to the eternal kingdom Christ has promised us. We need to bless those who have harmed us and bless those who have persecuted us, embracing the spiritual reality—they have only empowered us in the Lord Jesus Christ. They may continue to think they have hurt us, but what they do not realize is that they are strengthening us more and more to do God's work.

At times, our lives will feel like the waters of the ocean as they crash upon the rocks, the current constantly tugging at our souls. We try to hold on, but eventually we are swept away, and back to the ocean we go. However, if we let go and let the Holy Spirit take us, He will guide us toward greater works and uplift our very souls.

THOUGHT PROVOKING

Could it be that during the hardest times in life our destiny is waiting to be revealed?

We grow spiritually by turning everything over to the Lord, letting him command our spirits and letting Him be the rudder of our lives. In Him and through Him, we claim the power of the Holy Spirit and can breathe in the coolness of His love and bask in His radiant joy.

II Chronicles 7:14

> *"If My people who are called by My name will humble themselves and pray and seek My face and turn from their wicked ways, then I will hear from heaven and will forgive their sin and heal their land."*

Christ paid the price of sin with His life. We have been bought with a price: The precious blood of Christ, a lamb without blemish and without spot. In the following scripture, Peter says, "He indeed was fore-ordained before the foundation of the world but was manifest in these last times for you."

1 Peter 1:19-23

"But with the precious blood of Christ, as of a lamb without blemish and without spot. He indeed was foreordained before the foundation of the world, but was manifest in these last times for you who through Him believe in God, who raised Him from the dead and gave Him glory, so that your faith and hope are in God. Since you have purified your souls in obeying the truth through the Spirit in sincere love of the brethren, love one another fervently with a pure heart, having been born again, not of corruptible seed but incorruptible, through the word of God which lives and abides forever,"

Furthermore, in verse 23 we learn that we have been *Born Again*, not of corruptible seed, but incorruptible, through the word of God which lives and abides forever.

Jesus promises us eternal life, grounded in His sacrificial offering and God's love. His message is for every one of us, whether we trust in him or not. God does not force His love upon us; it is His gift to us. It is our decision to receive the gift and place our trust in Him alone for salvation.

2 Peter 3:9

"The Lord is not slack concerning His promise, as some count slackness, but is longsuffering toward us, not willing that any should perish but that all should come to repentance."

John 3:16

"For God so loved the world that He gave His only begotten Son, that whoever believes in Him should not perish but have everlasting life."

How to begin the journey of living a fulfilled life is quite simple—make the decision to unplug from worldly lusts and plug into God's loving and forgiving power.

CHALLENGE QUESTIONS

Why is water baptism such an important element in plugging into God's power strip?

What does it mean to be baptized with the Holy Spirit?

What is meant by "baptism with fire?"

Have you invited Christ into your heart and embraced Him as the Lord of your life?

Have you been water baptized?

Have you been baptized with the Holy Spirit and fire?

Would you agree that God does not want us to perish but have everlasting life?

CHAPTER VI

PLUGGING INTO GOD
THROUGH THE TRINITY

"Jesus said to him, 'You shall love the Lord your God with all your heart, with all your soul, and with all your mind.'" (Matthew 22:37)

"You should love your God with all your heart, with all your soul, and with all your strength." (Deuteronomy 6:5)

The three distinct persons of the Trinity are God the Father, God the Son, and God the Holy Spirit, and in Genesis 1:27 we learn, "God created man in His own image; in the image of God He created him; male and female He created them."

God the Father is all encompassing, and to know Him is to know His heart. God the Son came to us in the physical and continues to be with us in the Living Word, and God the Holy Spirit is a person sent by the Father and is spiritually present in all of nature and within the heart of every true believer.

*The Reverend Matthew Carr states, "**Heart** includes the emotions, will, purpose; **soul**, the spiritual faculties; **mind**, the intellect, the thinking faculty."[12]*

In view of the foregoing, the three primary ways we plug into God through a loving relationship are:

- Emotionally through our hearts, which include our emotions, wills, and purposes
- Spiritually through our souls and spiritual faculties
- Physically through our minds, intellect, and bodies.

All three are interwoven, and we are endued with God's triune character in our living being.

Genesis 1:27

"God created man in His own image; in the image of God He created him; male and female He created them."

This chapter is meant to be a companion to the previous chapter so I would like you think about the following as you continue reading: water baptism is a physical act, baptism of the Holy Spirit is a spiritual act, and baptism by fire has an impact on our emotional state.

By plugging into God through His triune nature, we avoid being perverted by the sins deep in our hearts. God imparts His spirit so we can discern good from evil, right from wrong, truth from lies, and fact from fiction. He provides a level of protection in the supernatural that allows us to judge the moral character of our human conduct. He longs to protect us from anyone or anything that intends to bring us harm.

---

12   Carr, Rev. Matthew 1881. Matthew XXII. The Cambridge Bible for Schools, edited by J.J.S. Perowne. Cambridge: At The University Press, 1881

PLUGGING IN PHYSICALLY

You plug in physically through baptism as you mindfully put your trust in Jesus Christ and acknowledge His sacrifice of body and blood for the atonement for your sins. You make a conscious, heartfelt effort to live for Him by making Him the Lord of your life. In Chapter Five, we covered baptism extensively and the important part baptism plays as we eternally plug into God. In this chapter, I want to challenge you to look at your own life and honestly evaluate where you are in your relationship with Christ.

THOUGHT PROVOKING

Have you been baptized? As a child? As an adult?

The Bible contains many examples where baptism was encouraged. The following are a few of them:

At Pentecost, Peter encouraged the people living in Jerusalem to be baptized.

Acts 2:38

"Then Peter said to them, 'Repent, and let every one of you be baptized in the name of Jesus Christ for the remission of sins, and you shall receive the gift of the Holy Spirit.'"

Paul, speaking in Rome, instructed his audience to embrace baptism. He taught that in baptism they were plugged into Christ's death leading to "newness of life."

Romans 6:3-4

"Or do you not know that as many of us as were baptized into Christ Jesus were baptized into His death? Therefore, we were buried with Him through baptism into death, that just as Christ was raised

*from the dead by the glory of the Father, even so we
also should walk in newness of life."*

In Galatians, Paul instructs us that the result of being baptized in Christ is that we become brothers and sisters in Christ. We are no longer divided across religious lines and no longer male or female because we have become one in Christ.

Galatians 3:26-28

"For you are all sons of God through faith in Christ Jesus. For as many of you as were baptized into Christ have put on Christ. There is neither Jew nor Greek, there is neither slave nor free, there is neither male nor female, for you are all one in Christ Jesus."

After Jesus' resurrection, He met with His disciples on a mountain in Galilee and gave them what has been called *The Great Commission.* He instructs them to make disciples and to baptize.

Matthew 28:19

"Go, therefore, and make disciples of all the nations, baptizing them in the name of the Father and of the Son and of the Holy Spirit",

A wonderful story is found in Acts 10, which I would encourage you to read in its entirety. For our purposes, I will condense the story to show the important part baptism plays in the lives of believers who have received a new revelation from the Lord.

Peter was staying with Simon the tanner in Joppa and was on the housetop when he fell into a trance. He had an encounter with God that would open his eyes that even Gentiles were worthy of God's grace. Twice during his trance, he heard a voice say, "What God has cleansed you must not call common." When Peter awoke, he had no idea what the vision meant until he encountered men who had been sent from a Centurion named Cornelius from Caesarea.

Four days before Peter's trance, Cornelius had an encounter with an angel who told him where Peter was staying and told him to send for him. In anticipation of Peter's arrival, Cornelius gathered all of his close friends and relatives. While Peter was sharing the good news of Jesus Christ, the Holy Spirit fell upon those in attendance. Peter then commands them to be baptized.

Acts 10:48

"And he commanded them to be baptized in the name of the Lord..."

THOUGHT PROVOKING

What do you think Peter learned from the vision?

Allow me to me share my personal baptism experience. Soon after renewing my vows of Lordship, which I will describe in detail in Chapter Nine, I had a series of dreams. One dream woke me around 4:30 in the morning—I was going to die in sixty days. The dream was extremely real, but there was no fear associated with it. I wrote in my journal that the dream must be referring to some form of spiritual death, not necessarily a physical death. However, just in case, I wrote in my journal how I wanted to be buried.

Being a member of a small group at the time, I decided to share the dream in the hope someone could interpret what it meant. However, after relating the dream, each person said, "Wow, I don't know what the Lord is saying." Not finding an answer, I chose to put the dream out of my mind.

Unknown to me at the time, our church was planning a baptism poolside at the same house where our Bible study was conducted. I had never been to a baptism where people were immersed in a swimming pool, so I decided to attend. When I arrived, I found out it was being held at my friend's house because he and his wife were to be baptized. Although we had been meeting regularly for several weeks, no one in our group mentioned they were planning to be baptized.

I was sitting alone near the pool when another member from our group, a feisty gal with blazing red hair, passed by and asked, "Are you getting baptized today?"

I snidely replied, "I've already been baptized."

She promptly rebutted, "Not since you've had a new understanding."

I hesitated for a moment and said, "You're right."

"Go talk to the pastor," she told me. I was not about to argue with her, so I approached the pastor and asked if I could be baptized.

He asked a series of questions about my relationship with Christ, and I must have answered correctly because he said, "Sure, you can be baptized."

My friend who owned the house overheard our conversation and said, "Come on. I have a bathing suit that will fit you."

I entered the waters of baptism right after my friend and his wife. As I emerged from the pool, a little voice in my mind said, "This is sixty days from the date that you had your dream."

I climbed out of the pool and said to the wife of my friend, "Do you remember the dream I told the group about?"

She said, "Yes, why?"

I said, "This is sixty days to the date." We both stood staring at one another, stunned.

To be sure, I went home and checked my journal. God had a special plan for me that day. However, what really impacted my life was the God of the Universe and Creator of everything known to man thought enough about me to meet me in a swimming pool in the backyard of a friend's house to tell me how much I meant to Him.

The experience still sends chills up my spine. I am not one to analyze dreams, but I now realize that God uses different ways to let us know that He loves us, cares about us, and has a plan for our lives. He had my attention: I had plugged into God physically through the waters of baptism.

Joel 2:28

"And it shall come to pass afterward That I will pour out My Spirit on all flesh; Your sons and your daughters shall prophesy, Your old men shall dream dreams, Your young men shall see visions."

PLUGGING IN SPIRITUALLY

We plug in spiritually through our soul and all of our spiritual faculties. When we put our trust in Christ and believe by faith in God's gift of salvation and the covering that gift provides, we are firmly plugged into God's power strip.

In the first chapter, we learned the importance of holding all thoughts captive to the obedience of Christ. When we consistently obey, we are acknowledging our trust in Christ, and He shields us from the strongholds, arguments, and everything else bent on our destruction.

2 Corinthians 10:4-6

"For the weapons of our warfare are not carnal but mighty in God for pulling down strongholds, casting down arguments and every high thing that exalts itself against the knowledge of God, bringing every thought into captivity to the obedience of Christ, and being ready to punish all disobedience when your obedience is fulfilled."

"Return to Sender" was a song popularized by Elvis Presley in the 1960s. The song is about a frustrated lover trying to reconnect with his love.

"Return to sender, address unknown
No such number, no such zone
We had a quarrel, a lover's spat
I write I'm sorry, but my letter keeps coming back."

The girl in the song had it right by opting to return the letter to the sender. I want to propose another meaning for the song, a spiritual meaning. Our enemy is constantly trying to remind us of our past. For us to plug into God spiritually, we must return all of our old tapes (past negative experiences) to the sender.

THOUGHT PROVOKING

How many times have you reached into the archives of your mind, pulled out an old tape of your past, and played it?

63

If you are like most people, when moments of depression or loneliness set in, you open your archives. It is like walking into a video store. The old tapes are neatly arranged and labeled. One row is labeled pity party, one is labeled depression, another lustful nature, and several rows are set aside for various addictions. Why live in the present when we can live in the past? After all, unlike real life, we can control what is on those tapes. Oh yes, we just splice in parts that are missing or edit out parts that we don't want to acknowledge. Don't you think it would be best to return those tapes to the sender, your spiritual enemy—Satan?

Let me share one of my old tapes with you. I was in the fifth grade. It was a beautiful day, not a cloud in the sky (spliced in). As I was walking to school, a car slowed, and the passenger rolled down the window (in those days not all cars had electric windows). The passenger, a good friend, asked if I would like a ride to school, to which I responded, "Of course." His mother dropped us off at a convenience store (no longer there) located on a corner near the school.

As we entered the store, I asked my friend, "Can I borrow some money, so I can buy a candy bar? I left my lunch money at home." He stated that he too had left his money at home. Not wanting to be denied the sweet delicacy, I strolled over to the candy section, casually put an Almond Joy candy bar on top of my books, and walked out.

To my dismay, the clerk gave chase and yelled to the crossing guard nearby that he had been robbed. You guessed it; I was caught red-handed. Then, I was taken to the jailhouse. How degrading to be thrown into jail, but even more degrading, I had been busted by a crossing guard. It was approximately 7:00 in the morning when the police called my parents. My father came to pick me up, and I could tell by the look on his face I was in real trouble.

The stay in jail in no way compared to the punishment I was to endure when we arrived home. I was instructed to go to my room and wait. There I sat, uneasy and waiting for my father, the silence deafening. Suddenly, the door swung open, and he crossed the room with his belt in hand. After being punished, my mother drove me back to school and escorted me in. Amazingly, everyone at school seemed to know about my experience. The so-called friend had proceeded to tell as many people as possible that I had been thrown in jail for stealing a candy bar.

How demoralizing that day was in the life of a little boy. Unknown to anyone at the time, that event planted a negative seed in my heart that would sprout and grow into my adult life—a seed of shame manifesting in low self-esteem, anger, defensiveness, and aggressiveness.

Now, you might be asking, "Why would you replay that tape?" Because when things were not going the right way, all I had to do is pull out that tape and blame my predicament on the store clerk, my father, and my friend. After all, they were the ones at fault for my shortcomings. If that clerk had not turned me in, if Dad had not hit me, and if my friend had not told anyone, everything would have been fine. I could have gone on stealing from the convenience store, and no one would have been the wiser. Instead, because of their abuse, they totally screwed up my life. At least, those are the lies a spiritual enemy would have me believe.

However, when I plugged into God spiritually, I was able to look at the situation in a different way. If I had never taken the candy bar, my friend would never have said anything, and there would have been no need for my father to punish me. Wow, that is an interesting and different perspective!

In other words, if I had controlled my behavior, if I had made the right choice, if I had listened to the voice of reason—the still, small voice that echoed, "Don't do it," – I could have been spared all the agony of that morning. We all hear the voice of reason prior to acting on sinful courses of action. Had I listened, the course of my life would have been altered and future years of my life affected in a positive way.

Sin damages a part of our souls, erodes our personalities, and taints our behavioral patterns. Not dealt with, it can fester like a virus, spread into other areas of our lives, and manifest later into greater sin.

The effect of sin is not positive, even though some good might come from it. Many of the other children at school had been robbing the convenience store. We joked about how easy it was. We even made it a game to see who could steal the most. Thus, when I was arrested, the authorities had no choice but to make me an example. They lowered the hammer, and I took on the punishment for all the other kids. However, as a result, we stopped stealing from that store. I became the sacrificial lamb, so to speak.

Sound familiar? Yes, I might have been the chosen vessel to save those schoolchildren from a life of crime. Quite possibly, because of my incarceration, some other child might have been spared a similar fate. As for me, I got everything I deserved and paid the consequence for my sin. Oh, one more thing; I cannot remember ever stealing another candy bar. God will bring good out of every situation if we place our love in Him.

Romans 8:28

"And we know that all things work together for good to those who love God, to those who are the called according to His purpose."

When we are plugged in spiritually, we are protected from our ignorance and more apt to hear the Lord's voice. Even if we fall prey to our sin, we are able to deal with issues immediately, learn from them, and avoid further destruction. We begin to develop a personal relationship on a spiritual level previously unknown to most people.

2 Corinthians 10:13-14

These things we also speak, not in words which man's wisdom teaches but which the Holy Spirit teaches, comparing spiritual things with spiritual. But the natural man does not receive the things of the Spirit of God, for they are foolishness to him; nor can he know them, because they are spiritually discerned.

THOUGHT PROVOKING

Do you agree that plugging in spiritually protects us from ourselves?

At one time, I was burdened with a groin pull, which hindered my ability to jog. One morning while I was out running, the pain flared. As I slowed and began to walk, the Lord spoke to me, "When the pain seems too great, remember in time it will pass, and when it does you will see that the pain remained in order to slow you down so I could prepare your path." Then I heard, "Keep putting one foot in front of the other, and you will make it home, but if you stop you won't make it."

Remaining spiritually plugged in will not only help us to endure our pain, but also it will strengthen us for the journey the Lord has us on. If we don't give up, in time we begin to understand that God allows adversity in our lives to make us stronger. Sometimes, it is there to steer us back onto the path He knows that is best for us. At other times, He is building our character in order to instill eternal hope.

Romans 5:3-5

"And not only that, but we also glory in tribulations, knowing that tribulation produces perseverance; and perseverance, character; and character, hope. Now hope does not disappoint because the love of God has been poured out in our hearts by the Holy Spirit who was given to us."

II Corinthians 12:9-10

"And He said to me, 'My grace is sufficient for you, for My strength is made perfect in weakness.' Therefore, most gladly I will rather boast in my infirmities, that the power of Christ may rest upon me. Therefore, I take pleasure in infirmities, in reproaches, in needs, in persecutions, in distresses for Christ's sake. For when I am weak, then I am strong."

If you are like most people, there are times you are in such a hurry that you miss His instruction. In my example above, the day before I had been asking for His instruction and direction for my life and purpose. His response was not exactly what I wanted to hear, but He was speaking loud and clear. Since I was plugged in spiritually, I embraced the lesson. His burden is light, and His yoke is easy. Yes, painful at times, but light and easy when we rest in Him knowing that He is preparing our path and leading us on life's journey.

Matthew 11:30

"For My yoke is easy and My burden is light."

God spiritually works in the hearts of men and women. Even when we doubt that He hears our cries. He is always at work clearing and preparing the path for the purposes He created us for, He will not be thwarted. Hebrews 13:8 teaches, "Jesus Christ is the same yesterday, today, and forever."

His plan and direction for our lives does not change. We are the ones who get in the way by taking shortcuts and thinking we can move the process along. In the end, as we look back, we can see clearly see where we got off His path, and if we look carefully, we can see where we re-entered His path and ultimately reached our destination.

He does not impose His will on us, but since He created us with a purpose, it would make sense that He has a will for each of us. When we plug into His spirit, He will reveal His purpose for us. The reason He created us unfolds, and as we pray for His wisdom and give into His guidance, our will comes into alignment with His will, our plans are established, and our paths become clear.

Proverbs 19:21

> *"Many are the plans in a person's heart, but it is the LORD's purpose that prevails." (NIV)*

THOUGHT PROVOKING

Where is your path leading? Do you trust fully in His will for your life? Are you praying that your will would line up with His will?

We also enter spiritual relationships with others. We might not know we are in spiritual relationship with one another because we cannot physically see the connection. However, when we are plugged into God's power strip, the unseen activity is constantly in motion.

We can use the example of our wireless world. Did you ever stop to think that God is the inventor of wireless technology? Many might think man invented it, but I quote Solomon who said in Ecclesiastes 1:9, "What has been will be again, what has been done will be done again. There is nothing new under the sun." We are using God's technology every day in our lives.

I hope that you are beginning to see how to tap into God's technology that already exists in nature by plugging into Him spiritually. Man has not invented anything that God has not already invented. If you are still having doubts about this theorem, let me pose an elementary example to make the point perfectly clear. Birds were created by God and were flying long before man ever left the ground; ergo, man didn't invent flying.

Spiritual principles work in a secular environment because of the *Spiritual Nature* of our Creator. He is all around us and is all encompassing in nature. We cannot see Him any more than we can see the air we breathe, but there is no denying the air's existence. His power flows freely, so in a sense when we are plugged into God spiritually, we are also plugged into to others in His Kingdom. God acts as the conduit by which we have meaningful relationships.

PLUGGING IN EMOTIONALLY

When you are honestly ready for your life to change, God knows and will guide you on your journey in such a way that you could never imagine. He will allow you to plug in emotionally through your heart, will, and conscious mind.

In the 1950's, there was a self-help course titled *Dynamic Man* developed by Robert Conklin, who instructed his students, "People change when they hurt enough that they have to change, learn enough that they want to change, receive enough that they are able to change."

THOUGHT PROVOKING

Which category do you fall into? Are you able to change?

The Holy Spirit was sent to us to provide an intimate relationship with the Father. He leads us on the path that God has purposed for us. God desires to connect us through the power of His Spirit so that we can identify and break free from the lies that echo in our minds. As we discern the voice of the Holy Spirit and walk alongside of Him, we find the joy that is missing when we are plugged into the world.

We have a spiritual enemy who attempts to heap on us condemnation that is born out of anger through lies and deception. In contrast, the Holy Spirit always brings conviction that is born out of love and provides positive instruction.

Conviction	**Condemnation**
Born out of love	Born out of anger
Delivered through positive instruction	Delivered through lies and deception

We all know fire is hot, and it burns. Imagine, if you will, a child reaching up to a hot stove and his mother slapping his hand to protect him from being burned. Unfortunately, some people witnessing the act might criticize her for slapping her child's hand. Our world has so bought into the enemy's lies and become deceived that some people might punish the mother for slapping her child's hand.

Yes, when ignorant of the facts, they might draw the wrong conclusion by saying she was being abusive. After all, who is she to hit her child? Without the proper knowledge and understanding of the truth, they would perceive this incident in the wrong light. They would be ignorant to the fact that she had saved her child from extreme agony and provided necessary instruction for his future. The slap always hurts, but in this example, it is the slap of conviction out of love, not the slap of condemnation out of anger.

As a child, I learned the hard way by picking up a scorching lamp on a dare. My family was having a picnic around a small lake, and as night approached, we lit portable lanterns. One of my cousins dared me to pick up one of the lamps by saying, "It won't hurt you."

I refused, so he said, "You're just scared."

I then heard someone say, "Don't pick it up it will burn you. Just ignore him."

Well, I ignored the warning, and before anyone could stop me, I grabbed the lantern by the handle. Thus, out of ignorance, I burned my hand to such a degree I had to have it treated and wrapped.

We all learn in different ways. However, the pain resulting from the conviction of the Holy Spirit hurts a lot less than the pain resulting from condemnation delivered through lies and deception. I had no idea the Holy Spirit was speaking through another individual, the one who warned me not to pick up the lantern. I failed to listen and paid a price. However, because of my experience, I now listen to the voice of reason. By the way, I have yet to pick up another hot lamp without insulating the handle.

Earlier in the book, we learned when Jesus ascended to the Father, He sent the Helper. John 16:5-7, "Nevertheless I tell you the truth. It is to your advantage that I go away, for if I do not go away, the Helper will not come to you…" The Holy Spirit came to us to bring conviction. He convicts those who are in sin, and He convicts us so that we learn of Jesus' righteousness and desire His righteousness in our own lives.

John 16:8-11

> *"And when He has come, He will convict the world of sin and of righteousness and of judgment: of sin because they do not believe in Me; of righteousness because I go to My Father, and you will see Me no more; of judgment because the ruler of this world is judged."*

Once we are plugged into God emotionally, we begin consciously to ask the Holy Spirit to search our hearts. We ask Him to expose all ungodly areas and sear our consciences with conviction to the point we desire to change. Our hearts are changed, and we have a firmer understanding of the truth. Eventually, when sin rises up, and it will, we are aware of His still, small voice as it echoes in our minds. Knowing it is the Holy Spirit bringing conviction, we embrace the remorseful pain in our hearts. We understand that we are not being condemned, but that the Holy Spirit is convicting us because we are operating outside of God's will. The Holy Spirit's conviction eventually leads us to repentance, which leads us to salvation.

Proverbs 6:27-28

> *"Can a man take fire to his bosom and his clothes not be burned? Can one walk on hot coals and his feet not be seared?"*

Romans 8:1-2

> *"There is, therefore, now no condemnation to those who are in Christ Jesus, who do not walk according to the flesh, but according to the Spirit. For the law of the Spirit of life in Christ Jesus has made me free from the law of sin and death."*

2 Corinthians 7:10

For godly sorrow produces repentance leading to salvation, not to be regretted, but the sorrow of the world produces death.

So, what is does it mean to truly repent? Frederick Fyvie Bruce was a well-known biblical scholar who instructed his students that to repent is to turn from sin toward God. In other words, repentance means to reverse direction, turn away from sin, and walk toward righteousness.

According to Bruce, "Repentance (metanoia, 'change of mind') involves a turning with contrition from sin to God; the repentant sinner is in the proper condition to accept the divine forgiveness."[13]

Imagine that you have been walking along a sinful path in life, and you are miserable. You know that the lifestyle you are living is stripping you of all you hold dear. As the weight of that conviction becomes unbearable, you hear a still, small voice say, "Why don't you just turn around and walk in the opposite direction." Suddenly, in your emotional state, you realize that you are experiencing conviction. You embrace the feeling knowing all you have to do is stop, turn around, and begin living according to God's Word.

In Luke 13:1-5, Jesus was instructing His disciples when some in attendance pointed to the sin of Galileans. Knowing the intent of their hearts, Jesus seized the opportunity to preach on the importance for all to repent. He pulls no punches, telling them that without repentance all are going to perish.

Luke 13:1-5

---

13   F. F. Bruce. *The Acts of the Apostles* [Greek Text Commentary], London: Tyndale, 1952, p. 97

> *"There were present at that season some who told Him about the Galileans whose blood Pilate had mingled with their sacrifices. And Jesus answered and said to them, 'Do you suppose that these Galileans were worse sinners than all other Galileans because they suffered such things? I tell you, no, but unless you repent, you will all likewise perish. Or those eighteen on whom the tower in Siloam fell and killed them, do you think that they were worse sinners than all other men who dwelt in Jerusalem? I tell you, no, but unless you repent, you will all likewise perish.'"*

The Greek word for "repent" in Luke is *metanoeō*, which means to think differently, reconsider.[14] To change one's mind for better, heartily to amend with abhorrence one's past sins. This type of repentance cuts to the core of our hearts, deep within our subconscious minds. This repentance leads to eternal salvation. We turn away from the wrong behavior and toward a right standing with the Lord.

Acts 3:19

> *"Repent therefore and be converted, that your sins may be blotted out, so that times of refreshing may come from the presence of the Lord."*

Ephesians 4:21-24

> *"If indeed you have heard Him and have been taught by Him, as the truth is in Jesus: that you put off, concerning your former conduct, the old man who grows corrupt according to the deceitful lusts and be renewed in the spirit of your mind and that you put*

---

14   Strong, James. 1894. Dictionary of the words in The Greek Testament. New York: Hunt & Eaton.

on the new man which was created according to God
in true righteousness and holiness."

Once we begin unplugging from our old habits, we need to learn to make confession. By confessing our transgressions, we silence the enemy found in our former conduct. From my own perspective, confession is an outward acknowledgment of our wrongful behavior, and repentance is an outward expressive action confirming our confession. When we faithfully confess our sins one to another, God is faithful to remove them completely from our hearts.

1 John 1:9

"If we confess our sins, He is faithful and just
to forgive us our sins and to cleanse us from all
unrighteousness."

James 5:16

"Confess your trespasses to one another and pray for
one another that you may be healed. The effective,
fervent prayer of a righteous man avails much."

THOUGHT PROVOKING

Have you felt the pain of conviction?

When you are ready to change, the Lord will bring you alongside others who are on a similar path. It has been my experience that He will join you with people who have had similar experiences which causes their counsel to resonate and encourage you on your journey more fully. He will bring you into these relationships in a variety of ways, some being more direct than others.

For example, let's assume you are visiting a counselor for the issues you are struggling with. The counselor offers you sound advice and adds, "Let me give you a number of someone I know who has gone through a similar experience. He can provide a perspective that only someone who has gone through what you are facing can provide."

At other times, He might introduce you to other brothers and sisters in Christ who share their stories, and you realize they have suffered the same thing you are going through. Spiritual counsel is much more effective coming from someone who has had a similar experience.

The Lord loves us, and if we will trust Him, He knows exactly what we need during our darkest times. He will plug us in emotionally to others to sharpen us.

I caution that men and women should not be intimately mentoring members of the opposite sex. I am not referring to professional counselors, but individuals God brings into our lives for accountability. If you are a man, God will bring you into accountability with another man. If you are a woman, He will introduce you to another woman.

Proverbs 27:17

"As iron sharpens iron, so a man sharpens the countenance of his friend."

It is worth noting that the word "man" used in this Proverb also means a woman. As we saw earlier in Genesis 1:27, when creating the world, God used the term "man" to denote both male and female, "So God created man in His own image; in the image of God, He created him; male and female He created them."

Allow me to share a personal experience how the Lord brought a person into my heart at just the right time. One Sunday morning, I was awakened, but it was a weird moment. I seemed to be both asleep and awake. A quiet voice was echoing in my head, "Read Deuteronomy."

The thought went through my mind, "I've read Deuteronomy, and that's a long book, I'm not getting up to read it."

Again, the voice spoke, "If you don't get up now, you won't have time to read Deuteronomy before going to church."

Well, I remember thinking to myself, "Okay already, I'll get up and read." I read the whole book before going off to church.

Deuteronomy 1:1

"These are the words which Moses spoke to all Israel on this side of the Jordan in the wilderness, in the plain opposite Suph, between Paran, Tophel, Laban, Hazeroth, and Dizahab."

The book of Deuteronomy is an account of Moses speaking to the Israelites before they cross over to the Promised Land. The book is all about obedience and the remembrance of how their forefathers had let God down. Reading, I was prompted to look at the patterns in my life. I realized I was not much different from the Israelites. I promptly asked the Lord to expose any areas of disobedience and enact a change in my heart.

The real significance of the dream would be the journey the Lord was about to take me on, a journey that I am still traveling today as I write this book.

THOUGHT PROVOKING

What journey has the Lord taken you on?

The next week, I met a man in our church congregation. At the time, I did not know anything about him. Later, I learned he was one of the elders of the church and was planning a mission trip to Cuba. He approached me one Sunday and said, "I feel like the Lord wanted me to ask you if you would join us on the mission trip. Before I could answer he said, "Oh, one more thing, the Lord told me to provide your support." I told him I would pray about the trip and get back to him.

Walking away somewhat stunned, I was thinking, "Is this guy for real?"

On that trip, God birthed a relationship that He would use to propel me on my spiritual journey. The church elder and I spent time with one another sharing our innermost thoughts. I felt relieved that there was someone who could relate to my journey. Instead of rebuking me, he listened, and a weight was removed from my shoulders. The Lord used this person to elevate me to a greater level of spiritual maturity.

When we returned from the trip, we continued to meet over the next few months holding each other accountable to a more righteous lifestyle. In time, we co-hosted a men's group that met every week for several years. Over the years, the Lord allowed us to touch many lives.

Without realizing it, I had plugged into the Lord emotionally through my conscious mind. He challenged me to read His word, I accepted the challenge, and a change took place in my heart. He then presented an opportunity for me to plug into an emotional relationship with another Christian with a similar background. Through that mentoring relationship, He brought the answer to my prayer, "Lord expose any areas of disobedience and enact a change in my heart."

So, as we learn to hear His voice and allow the conviction of the Holy Spirit to expose areas of our hearts that need to be cleansed, we are encouraged to repent, turning away from the sin to the protection of the Holy Spirit. As we make confession one to another, we are strengthened in our conviction to live a more righteous lifestyle. We also have someone to hold us accountable to that lifestyle.

Deuteronomy 30:19-20

"I call heaven and earth as witnesses today against you that I have set before you life and death, blessing and cursing; therefore, choose life, that both you and your descendants may live, that you may love the LORD *your God, that you may obey His voice, and that you may cling to Him, for He is your life and the length of your days, and that you may dwell in the land which the* LORD *swore to your fathers, to Abraham, Isaac, and Jacob, to give them."*

The Helper, His Holy Spirit, will protect us and empower us to fulfill our God-given destiny. God created us with free will; therefore, the choice is ours. If we are not willing to acknowledge Christ's deity and omnipresence, then we are being ignorant and are relegated to a life void of an intimate relationship with Him.

CHALLENGE QUESTIONS

How are we to love the Father according to the great commandment?

Has there been a time when you reached into the archives of your mind and played a hurtful tape from your past?

What impact did that tape have on your life?

What is the difference between conviction and condemnation?

What is the importance of true repentance?

Why is it important to confess your sins one to another?

Why should the book of Deuteronomy be mandatory reading in the life of a Christian?

Give some examples how God has plugged you into other Christians.

How does your thought life affect your spiritual walk?

CHAPTER VII

PLUGGED INTO GOD
THROUGH PRAYER

"Now in the morning, having risen a long while before daylight, He went out and departed to a solitary place, and there He prayed." (Mark 1:35)

Jesus understood the importance of maintaining personal fellowship with God and did so through prayer. Most often, He met with the Father early in the morning or off by himself. Jesus' days were filled with people longing to get close to him. His disciples constantly fed off His wisdom and the multitudes came to Him to be healed. He understood that to be alone with God meant getting away from the distractions of life. He set the example for every believer. Jesus Christ was well aware of His power source and drew upon it daily for substance and strength.

Luke 5:16

"So He Himself often withdrew into the wilderness and prayed."

Luke 6:12

"Now it came to pass in those days that He went out to the mountain to pray, and continued all night in prayer to God."

Matthew 14:23

"And when He had sent the multitudes away, He went up on the mountain by Himself to pray. Now when evening came, He was alone there."

Matthew 26:36

"Then Jesus came with them to a place called Gethsemane, and said to the disciples, 'Sit here while I go and pray over there.'"

King David in the Bible was a leader of people and a mighty warrior. He was the one who slew Goliath when all the other mighty warriors cowered in fear. How did David gain direction and strength? He spent time with God in the morning.

Psalm 5:3

"My voice You shall hear in the morning, O LORD; In the morning I will direct it to You, and I will look up."

Psalm 143:8

"Cause me to hear Your loving kindness in the morning, for in You do I trust; Cause me to know

*the way in which I should walk, for I lift up my soul
to You."*

By following the example set by Jesus and David, the most important way for us to plug in and stay plugged in is to give God the first fruits of our days. In doing so, we position ourselves to hear His voice and receive direction for our days and for our lives.

THOUGHT PROVOKING

How many people do you know who faithfully spend the first part of their day with the Lord?

Our time is a precious commodity, one we do not let go of easily. So why is it when things go wrong, we do not think twice about asking God to deliver us, but when it comes to spending time with Him, we are reluctant? Shouldn't we be intentional about scheduling time with God?

I have heard many excuses over the issue of scheduling time with God. Some contend, "I don't have a set time because I spend time with God throughout the day; I am constantly in prayer." Others say, "The demands of my spouse, children, and job make it hard to consistently meet with God, especially in the morning."

We all have demands on our time. The Lord knows our schedules better than anyone. However, the sinful nature within each of us might be offering these excuses to keep us from spending precious, personal time with our Father. Interestingly enough, not one person I have spoken with denies that they function better as a direct result of devoting time in the morning to meet with the Lord.

If you have children, you can get a sense of how God must feel. So often we long to be with our children, and when they take the time out of their schedules to initiate spending time with us, we are elated. However, when they ignore us and take us for granted, we are grieved.

I challenge you to think that if we are created in God's image that He too is grieved when we choose not to spend time with Him or when we make a weak effort to do so.

One of my friends had a son away at school, and communication didn't appear to be high on his son's priority list. My friend left messages, but never received a return call. He wondered why. On one occasion, he received notification that there was a voice mail from his son's number. He related his excitement, "I thought my son had actually returned my call." However, upon retrieving the message, he heard his own voice. It was the message he had left days earlier being kicked back. He became frustrated as a feeling of despair swept over him. He wondered if his son just did not care. Later, he learned that his son hadn't listened to any of his voice messages because he had lost his phone and was too scared to let his dad know.

What is the point in telling you this story? One morning in my quiet time with the Lord, it suddenly occurred to me that the same thing happens with our Father in heaven. When we fail to spend dedicated prayer time with the Lord, we might not hear Him speaking or confuse His messages with the idle chatter somewhere deep in our subconscious mind.

God is always speaking to us, leaving messages. However, oftentimes we do not pick them up, and we do not return His calls. Like my friend, God's Spirit becomes grieved.

Ephesians 4:30-32

> "And do not grieve the Holy Spirit of God, by whom you were sealed for the day of redemption. Let all bitterness, wrath, anger, clamor, and evil speaking be put away from you, with all malice. And be kind to one another, tenderhearted, forgiving one another, even as God in Christ forgave you."

We might be plugged into God and the communication link available, but we are at risk when we don't turn on our phone and listen. Turning our phone on is akin to spending time with God. When we make our time with the Lord a priority, we are acknowledging His manifold presence. Further, prayer creates a sacred bond where The Lord becomes the center of our lives.

THOUGHT PROVOKING

What is the best way to hear God speaking?

We will all face challenges in life. However, it is the instruction we receive through personal fellowship with the Lord that gives us the strength and direction to face those challenges. The Father longs to spend time with us, to communicate with us, to teach and instruct us. He longs for us to stay plugged into His power through prayer.

At the beginning of Jesus' ministry, He delivered the famous sermon on the mount in which he provided extensive instruction about how to live. In Matthew 6:5-13, we read that Jesus was very intentional about how we should pray. That prayer became known as the *Lord's Prayer*.

> *"'And when you pray, you shall not be like the hypocrites. For they love to pray standing in the synagogues and on the corners of the streets that they may be seen by men. Assuredly, I say to you, they have their reward. But you, when you pray, go into your room, and when you have shut your door, pray to your Father who is in the secret place, and your Father who sees in secret will reward you openly. And when you pray, do not use vain repetitions as the heathen do, for they think that they will be heard for their many words. "Therefore, do not be like them, for your Father knows the things you have need of before you ask Him. In this manner, therefore, pray:*
>
> *Our Father in heaven,*
>
> *Hallowed be Your name.*
>
> *Your kingdom come.*
>
> *Your will be done*
>
> *On earth as it is in heaven.*
>
> *Give us this day our daily bread.*
>
> *And forgive us our debts (trespasses/sin),*
>
> *As we forgive our debtors.*
>
> *And do not lead us into temptation,*
>
> *But deliver us from the evil one.*
>
> *For Yours is the kingdom and the power and the glory forever. Amen."*

We also learn in Luke 11:1-4 that Jesus responded to His Apostles with the same prayer when asked about how to pray, "Now it came to pass, as He was praying in a certain place, when He ceased, that one of His disciples said to Him, "Lord, teach us to pray, as John also taught his disciples." Jesus responded by giving them the same *Lord's Prayer* as he did in Matthew.

BREAKING DOWN THE LORD'S PRAYER

The prayer begins with a preface, moves into petition, and concludes with a doxology. The Lord's prayer is not intended to be prayed in habitual repetition, but continually throughout the day, more often in the recesses of your heart, that secret place that only you and the Lord can enter. He already knows what you need, but His prayer puts you in a posture to receive His blessings.

THE PREFACE
"Our Father in Heaven" - We address the all-mighty creator who is the Alpha and the Omega. He has no beginning and has no end. He spoke our world into existence, and His Kingdom continues to grow. Earlier in this writing, we learned about Dark Energy and how we live in a runaway universe where the most distant observable galaxies are racing away from us at breakneck speeds. As mere humans, to grasp the enormity of The Father's presence and His awesome power is impossible.

THE PETITIONS
"Hallowed be Your name" - He is Holy and set apart. We consecrate our lives to Him. He purifies us from all sin. Philip Crannell, an American theologian, once said, "To 'hallow the name' includes not only the inward attitude and outward action of profound reverence and active praise, but also that personal godliness, loving obedience and aggressive Christlikeness, which reveal the presence of God in the life, which is His true earthly glory."[15]

"Your kingdom come; Your will be done; On earth as it is in heaven" - We ask for His kingdom to come and His will be done in our earthly domain. Here we are acknowledging His dominion and His purpose. We cry out

---

15   Quote by *Philip Wendell Crannell,*

asking for Him to cover us with His supreme authority and that our purposes would line up with His purposes for our lives. We are inviting His heavenly realm to rain down on our earthly realm and provide His Divine covering over our lives.

"Give us this day our daily bread" - We long for the Lord to feed us and sustain us spiritually throughout the day. We will face many trials and tribulations, and we need His spiritual nourishment. The word Jesus used for "daily" is *epioúsios* and is only referenced in the Bible on the two occasions when Jesus was teaching how to pray. Each day is new, and He etches on our hearts a hunger and thirst for His righteousness. Other places in the Bible we learn about the shewbread, which is a symbol of our continued dependence upon God our Father. As we seek the face of God, He not only remains in our presence, but we are nourished by him throughout the day in our relationship with Jesus Christ.

"And forgive us our debts" - We ask for the forgiveness of our debts (trespasses/sins) and in turn agree to forgive our debtors of their trespasses/sins. This part of the prayer should be obvious to us, but so often we desire to be forgiven, yet want to hold on to our grievances against others. Jesus understands that we struggle with His instruction on forgiveness, so he felt it was important to explain further the concept to us in Matthew 6:14,

> *For if you forgive men their trespasses, your heavenly*
> *Father will also forgive you. But if you do not forgive*
> *men their trespasses, neither will your Father forgive*
> *your trespasses.*

To harbor resentment toward someone is to be in bondage to that person. Jesus desires for us to be set free from the bondage of unforgiveness by acknowledging that He paid the price for all sin.

"And do not lead us into temptation; But deliver us from the evil one" - At first this portion of the prayer doesn't seem to make sense. Why would He lead us into temptation? It is important to read Jesus' words in the proper context. As we previously looked at in Chapter three the Bible instructs us in James,

James 1:13

> *"Let no one say when he is tempted, 'I am tempted by God"; for God cannot be tempted by evil, nor does He Himself tempt anyone.'"*

When we ask God to lead us in our daily lives, we shouldn't fear that He would lead us into temptation but rejoice that He steers us clear from the evil that so easily ensnares us. We are the ones who succumb to temptation, and God is the one who provides a way out from the evil of that temptation.

1 Corinthians 10:13

> *"No temptation has overtaken you except such as is common to man; but God is faithful, who will not allow you to be tempted beyond what you are able, but with the temptation will also make the way of escape, that you may be able to bear it".*

God delivers us from evil and in doing so draws us or leads us into a more intimate relationship with Him. "No" can be a difficult word to hear and often is a difficult word to say. When we say no to temptation the Holy Spirit acting on God's behalf leads us not into temptation but away from the evil one, and if away from the evil one, then it would make sense that we are being led closer to God, to a closer relationship with our Father.

THE DOXOLOGY

"For Yours is the kingdom and the power and the glory forever" - We exalt God by acknowledging His Divinity and in doing so ignite our passion for Him. David made a similar petition when he addressed the Lord before his people in 1 Chronicles 29:10-20. Verses 10 and 11 set the tone and ignited the hearts of the people.

1 Chronicles 29:10-11

"Therefore David blessed the Lord before all the assembly; and David said: 'Blessed are You, Lord God of Israel, our Father, forever and ever. Yours, O Lord, is the greatness, The power and the glory, The victory and the majesty, for all that is in heaven and in earth is Yours. Yours is the kingdom, O Lord, and You are exalted as head over all.'"

Earlier in the prayer, we invited His Kingdom, and surely, we expect Him to come in power full of His glory. Now, close your eyes and recite these final words out loud. Do so with an expectant heart knowing that God hears you and wants to illuminate your soul, "For Yours is the kingdom and the power and the glory forever."

I encourage you to cry out to the Lord, thank the Lord, trust the Lord, and add your own petitions to His prayer.

John 14:13-14

"And whatever you ask in My name, that I will do, that the Father may be glorified in the Son. If you ask anything in My name, I will do it."

In closing say, "Father, I pray all this in the mighty name of my Lord and Savior, Jesus Christ. Amen." For we want to give Him all the glory for His wonderful sacrifice for our sins and for sending His Holy Spirit to live and work in our hearts. The word "Amen," seals the prayer as if to say "so it be" and is an expression of our absolute trust in the Lord.

When reciting the Lord's Prayer, or any prayer for that matter, take your time knowing that there is power in the spoken word. His desire is to have an intimate relationship with you through your prayer life. Don't give up when you are facing tribulation and remember His Holy Spirit is always available to comfort you. God is worthy of all our praise.

Luke 11:9-13

'So I say to you, ask, and it will be given to you; seek, and you will find; knock, and it will be opened to you. For everyone who asks receives, and he who seeks finds, and to him who knocks it will be opened. If a son asks for bread from any father among you, will he give him a stone? Or if he asks for a fish, will he give him a serpent instead of a fish? Or if he asks for an egg, will he offer him a scorpion? If you then, being evil, know how to give good gifts to your children, how much more will your heavenly Father give the Holy Spirit to those who ask Him!'"

CHALLENGE QUESTIONS

What is the importance of maintaining personal fellowship with God through prayer?

Where and when did Jesus meet with His Father?

How did David gain direction and strength?

What do we receive when spend the first fruits of our day with God?

Why do we pray?

What kind of bond does prayer create between God and us?

What instruction did Jesus give His disciples about prayer?

What are the three primary parts of the Lord's prayer?

What are the final words of the Lord's prayer?

Why are those words important?

CHAPTER VIII

PLUGGED INTO GOD THROUGH THE WORD

"And the Word became flesh and dwelt among us, and we beheld His glory, the glory as of the only begotten of the Father, full of grace and truth. John bore witness of Him and cried out, saying, "This was He of whom I said, 'He who comes after me is preferred before me, for He was before me.'" And of His fullness we have all received, and grace for grace. For the law was given through Moses, but grace and truth came through Jesus Christ." (John 1:14-17)

God is our Creator, and He loves us beyond what our human intelligence can comprehend. We come to know and understand Him more deeply as we read and inculcate His Word into our being. The Word comes alive within us. We learn from John the Baptist in the scripture above that Jesus is the Word made flesh. We should be plugging into the written Word daily, filtering everything through Him, making Him our ultimate authority and accountability and truly loving Him from the heart. He longs to provide covering for His children.

THOUGHT PROVOKING

Do you live for Him every day? Do you filter everything through Him? Is He your ultimate authority and accountability? Do you really love Him?

Staying plugged into God by daily reading His word allows you to grasp the revelation contained therein. As you read the Word with an understanding of His love, it will come to life and feed you with spiritual food you have never known. How profound to think that Jesus longs to come into your life through the Word.

As a man born into a fallen world, Jesus provided an example for us as He stayed plugged into God as the living Word. In the following scripture, Jesus spent forty days and nights in the wilderness fasting, only to emerge hungry and faced with Satan's temptations.

Matthew 4:1-3

"Then Jesus was led up by the Spirit into the wilderness to be tempted by the devil. And when He had fasted forty days and forty nights, afterward He was hungry. Now, when the tempter came to Him, he said, 'If You are the Son of God, command that these stones become bread.'"

Jesus responded to Satan's attack by quoting Deuteronomy 8:3,

Matthew 4:4

"But He answered and said, It is written, 'Man shall not live by bread alone, but by every word that proceeds from the mouth of God.'"

THOUGHT PROVOKING

What is the purpose of sustenance?

The Word serves to provide sustenance, to convict, and to teach. Furthermore, it is the pathway of our understanding to God's vision for our life. Sustenance provides nourishment to the soul by feeding us with the Word and thus keeping us connected to the Rock, which is Jesus Christ.

1 Corinthians 10: 1-4

"Moreover, brethren, I do not want you to be unaware that all our fathers were under the cloud, all passed through the sea, all were baptized into Moses in the cloud and in the sea, all ate the same spiritual food, and all drank the same spiritual drink. For they drank of that spiritual Rock that followed them, and that Rock was Christ."

Conviction identifies the sin within us or the issues God desires to bring to our attention. However, most importantly, through His Word, He reveals the thoughts and intents of our hearts.

Hebrews 4:12

"For the word of God is living and powerful and sharper than any two-edged sword, piercing even to the division of soul and spirit and of joints and marrow, and is a discerner of the thoughts and intents of the heart."

THOUGHT PROVOKING

How does the Word teach us?

The Word provides biblical instruction on how to live our lives and become more like Christ. God inspires us to look at our lives and to correct those areas that do not line up with His Word. He inspires us through the scriptures. As the Word comes alive in our hearts, He brings the necessary correction so that we don't waiver along the way.

He continually provides instruction, thereby equipping us for life's journey. Earlier, we learned in 2 Timothy 3:16 that, "All Scripture is given by inspiration of God and is profitable for doctrine, for reproof, for correction, for instruction in righteousness." However, verse seventeen tells us what the Lord's desire is, "…that the man of God may be complete, thoroughly equipped for every good work."

Ephesians 2:10

"For we are his workmanship, created in Christ Jesus for good works, which God prepared beforehand, that we should walk in them."

Through God's Word, He testifies that we are His workmanship, deliberately crafted, and He provides each of us with a purpose in Christ. God longs to reveal His love for us in order to give us a future and a hope through Christ, the Word.

Jeremiah 29:11

"For I know the thoughts that I think toward you, says the Lord, thoughts of peace and not of evil, to give you a future and a hope."

Jesus Christ, through the Word, longs to come into our hearts and actively speak to us on God's behalf. We find ourselves drawn to certain scriptures more so than others. Those scriptures will confirm the inherent qualities that God placed in our hearts while we were in our mother's womb. The more time we spend in the Word the more we connect with God's vision for our lives.

Jeremiah 1:5

"Before I formed you in the womb, I knew you; Before you were born, I sanctified you…"

The devil, Satan, on the other hand, attempts to trick us through deception. In the next few verses, we will see how Satan continually attempted to trick Jesus by distorting the Word when our Lord was at His weakest.

Matthew 4:5-11

"Then the devil took Him up into the holy city, set Him on the pinnacle of the temple, and said to Him, 'If You are the Son of God, throw Yourself down. For it is written, 'He shall give His angels charge over you, and in their hands they shall bear you up, lest you dash your foot against a stone.' Jesus said to him, '"It is written again, 'You shall not tempt the LORD your God.'" Again, the devil took Him up on an exceedingly high mountain and showed Him all the kingdoms of the world and their glory. And he said to Him, 'All these things I will give You if You will fall down and worship me.' Then Jesus said to him, "Away with you, Satan! For it is written, 'You shall worship the LORD your God, and Him only you shall serve.'" Then, the devil left Him, and behold, angels came and ministered to Him."

In Satan's ignorance, he thought he could catch Jesus off guard. How did Jesus respond? He spoke the truth direct from His heart. The Word came out as naturally as breathing. Jesus did not have to open a scroll to know what to say.

Unfortunately, we are not born with the Word deeply imbedded in our hearts. Therefore, we must spend time reading, studying, and memorizing the Word. Our spiritual education will accelerate as we ask Him to reveal the wisdom contained in scripture.

James 1: 5-6

"If any of you lacks wisdom, let him ask of God, who gives to all liberally and without reproach, and it will

be given to him. But let him ask in faith, with no doubting, for he who doubts is like a wave of the sea driven and tossed by the wind."

THOUGHT PROVOKING

Have you been praying in faith, expecting to receive?

Over time, just like Christ's experience in the wilderness, our faith will become stronger, and we will automatically replace the lies of the enemy with the truth.

Romans 10:17

"So then faith comes by hearing, and hearing by the word of God."

As we develop the discipline of reading His Word on a consistent basis, the Word will permeate our souls, dig deep into our hearts, and guide and protect us from the sin contained therein. We will gain wisdom and understanding about life's issues and how to deal with them and come to identify with the vision God has for us.

Psalm 119:9-11

"How can a young man cleanse his way? By taking heed according to Your Word. With my whole heart I have sought You; oh, let me not wander from Your commandments! Your Word I have hidden in my heart that I might not sin against you."

Proverbs 4:5-7

"Get wisdom! Get understanding! Do not forget, nor turn away from the words of my mouth. Do not

forsake her, and she will preserve you; love her, and she will keep you. Wisdom is the principal thing; therefore, get wisdom. And in all your getting, get understanding."

As we plug into God through the Word, His Word dwells within us richly and will never pass away.

Colossians 3:16

"Let the word of Christ dwell in you richly in all wisdom, teaching and admonishing one another in psalms and hymns and spiritual songs, singing with grace in your hearts to the Lord."

Matthew 24:35

"Heaven and earth will pass away, but My words will by no means pass away."

I encourage you to search for and create a list of scriptures so when you feel you are being attacked spiritually you will be prepared to speak the Word of truth, *"For the word of God is living and powerful, and sharper than any two-edged sword..."*

The following topics are common to us all. I have provided a few scriptures you can choose from. However, the Bible is full of inspiration, direction, and wisdom for any situation you may be dealing with.

ACCUSATORY ATTACKS
Matthew 5:11; Isaiah 54:17; James 1:2-4; Proverbs 19:9; Psalm 109:2

ANGER ISSUES
Ephesians 4:26; Proverbs 29:11; Proverbs 15:1; James 1:19-20; Ephesians 4:31

ANXIETY
Philippians 4:6-8; 1 Peter 5:7; Proverbs 12:25; Matthew 6:25-34; 1 Peter 5:6-7

COMPLACENCY
Proverbs 1:32; Revelation 3:15-16; Proverbs 13:4; Zephaniah 1:12 2; Kings 19:28

COVETOUSNESS
Colossians 3:5; Luke 12:15; Ephesians 5:5; Hebrews 13:5; Exodus 20:17

DECEPTIVE ATTACKS
1 John 4:1; James 4:7; 1 Timothy 4:1; John 8:44; Ephesians 6:12

DEPRESSIVE THOUGHTS
1 Kings 19:1-21; 1 Corinthians 10:13; Revelation 1:1-20; 2 Corinthians 10:5; 2 Corinthians 4:16-18

FALSE HUMILITY
Philippians 2:3; James 4:10; 1 Peter 5:5; Colossians 2:18; Colossians 3:12

FEAR ISSUES
1 John 4:18; 2 Timothy 1:7; Isaiah 41:10; John 14:27; Psalm 27:1

FINANCIAL STRESS
Philippians 4:19; Proverbs 22:7; Philippians 4:6-7; Matthew 6:33; Proverbs 3:5-6

HEALTH ISSUES
Psalm 46:1-3; Isaiah 57:18; Jeremiah 30:17; Psalm 41:3; Psalm 18:2

INSECURE FEELINGS
Philippians 4:6; Romans 12:1-2; Romans 8:28-39; Isaiah 26:3; Psalm 23:1-6

LONELINESS
Isaiah 41:10; Matthew 28:20; Deuteronomy 31:6; Psalm 27:10; Genesis 2:18

LUSTFUL THOUGHTS
Matthew 5:28; Colossians 3:5; 1 Corinthians 10:31; Matthew 5:27; Proverbs 6:25

PORNOGRAPHY
1 Corinthians 6:18-20; 1 Corinthians 10:13; 1 John 2:16; Psalm 119:37; 1 Corinthians 6:18

PRIDEFULNESS
Proverbs 11:2; Proverbs 16:18; Proverbs 29:23; Proverbs 8:13; James 4:6

REJECTION
Psalm 34:17-20; John 15:18; 1 Peter 2:4; Psalm 27:10; 1 Peter 5:7

SELFISHNESS
Philippians 2:3-4; 2 Timothy 3:2-4; 1 John 3:17; 1 Corinthians 10:24; 1 Corinthians 13:4-6

STRESS
Psalm 55:22; John 14:27; Psalm 118:5-6; Matthew 11:28-30; James 1:12

TEMPTATION
1 John 1:9; John 3:16; Revelation 20:14; Revelation 12:9; 1 John 2:1

CHALLENGE QUESTIONS

Who is the Word?

What does the Word provide for God's children?

How did Jesus respond to Satan's temptations in the wilderness?

How does spiritual food provide sustenance for our souls?

What life lessons have you learned through biblical instruction?

What is your favorite scripture?

How does Satan attempt to trick us?

As our faith grows stronger, what do we replace the lies of the enemy with?

Have you written out your list of scriptures to ward off attacks of the enemy?

CHAPTER IX

꙳ ꙳ ꙳

PLUGGED INTO GOD
THROUGH COMMUNITY

"Now, therefore, you are no longer strangers and foreigners, but fellow citizens with the saints and members of the household of God," (Ephesians 2:19)

A nother way we plug into God is by spending time in fellowship with other believers through discipleship and corporate worship. We do so by joining a church family through which we have access to personal relationships with like-minded individuals.

Growing up, we learned the hard way that we are who we hang with, and that bad character corrupts good character. As we mature, this principle becomes more and more obvious. Many of the consequences we have paid or might still be paying are a result of hanging out with the wrong person or group of people.

I Corinthians 15:33-34

"Do not be deceived: 'Evil company corrupts good habits.' Awake to righteousness, and do not sin, for some do not have the knowledge of God. I speak this to your shame."

When we are plugged into God, He will plug us into the proper church family and into the proper relationships. His desire is that we would grasp the spiritual principle of being one with Him through a body of believers. God will use the family members according to their gifts to accomplish great things for His kingdom.

Romans 12:5

"So we, who are many, are one body in Christ, and individually members one of another."

When we allow God to connect us in spiritual family, we begin to see how each person has a part to play in the success of that family. But, if you are like most people, you have been frustrated by all the talk on finding your purpose, especially if you have not been able to discover yours.

THOUGHT PROVOKING

What is your God given purpose or part you are to fulfill within family?

When we actively show up and function out of the sincerity of our heart, our purpose becomes evident to those around us. If we are careful to listen, they will begin to affirm our purpose. Eventually, we will discover how our purpose is directly linked to the part we play in that family, and we grow spiritually.

Of course, it is up to us to stay in the game and not let the cares of the world weigh us down.

Hebrews 10:24-25

"And let us consider one another in order to stir up love and good works, not forsaking the assembling of ourselves together, as is the manner of some, but exhorting one another and so much the more as you see the Day approaching."

Contributing according to our gifts should not be hard for us to embrace, after all, we have all played a part in our natural families. We know that when all members play their parts and function together the family prospers, and when family members act independent of the family, all family members suffer.

In sports, when the proper team is put on the field and all players are functioning according to their gifts, the team will be successful. Everyone on a team has a part to play, and if one team member fails to execute, the team fails to accomplish the goal set before them.

When God joins you to a spiritual family, you have a part to play. The only decision you need to make is to attend and get involved. In other words, get off the bench and get into the game. When we get in the game and see how each member is important to the overall family, we will gain revelation about how it is going to be when we join the Lord in Heaven.

THOUGHT PROVOKING

Are you living the same Monday through Saturday as you are on Sunday?

Unfortunately, many people have been harmed by the church, so there will always be Christians who have become unplugged or are not properly plugged in. As a result, they have become spiritually "hogtied." They become restricted in their walk with God.

One time I was doing business with a fellow Christian, and I became suspicious of his actions. After what would be our last meeting, I asked, "Do you separate your Christian life from your business life?"

His response was startling. He said, "Yes, I do because so often in business, I have been burned by other Christians." Well, in the deal we were involved in, he burned my partner and me.

For this reason, before entering relationships with other Christians, you should know at what level they are plugged into God. Not everyone in church will be properly plugged in. Some are cultural Christians that are just going through the motions. Ask yourself if they are truly plugged into God or just paying lip service.

- Do they play an active and consistent part in the church, or are they only attending on occasion?
- Are they active in a home group or other small group within the church?

- Are they meeting with or open to meeting with two or three other Christian men or women who are members of their church?

If not, you might be putting yourself at risk if you seek their personal counsel or enter into a business relationship with them.

2 Corinthians 6:14-15

"Do not be unequally yoked together with unbelievers. For what fellowship has righteousness with lawlessness? And what communion has light with darkness? And what accord has Christ with Belial? Or what part has a believer with an unbeliever?"

THOUGHT PROVOKING

Aren't we called to spend time with non-believers?

When we are plugged in through our spiritual family, we learn to function in the world without being of the world. God still longs to connect us to those who are not Christians, to use us as conduits in order that one-day they might decide to plug in.

It is always important to know whom you are doing life with, because you will most definitely be plugged in with them at some level. There will be times when you must do business with or function with those who are in the world. Pray that the Lord will guide you in all your endeavors. Make sure you are spiritually covered.

John 17:15-17

"I do not pray that You should take them out of the world, but that You should keep them from the evil one. They are not of the world, just as I am not of the world. Sanctify them by Your truth. Your word is truth."

Jesus Christ provided the perfect example how to live a life while being plugged into God. He walked out His talk here on earth. However, He didn't isolate Himself from the world full of sinful men and women. He embraced them in love although He knew they were unplugged from His eternal blessing.

Luke 5:27-32

"After these things, He went out and saw a tax collector named Levi, sitting at the tax office. And He said to him, 'Follow Me.' So he left all, rose up, and followed Him. Then Levi gave Him a great feast in his own house. And there were a great number of tax collectors and others who sat down with them. And their scribes and the Pharisees complained against His disciples, saying, 'Why do You eat and drink with tax collectors and sinners?' Jesus answered and said to them, 'Those who are well have no need of a physician, but those who are sick. I have not come to call the righteous, but sinners, to repentance.'"

THOUGHT PROVOKING

Can the created fully understand the creator?

It is one thing to confess Jesus' death and resurrection, but it is entirely another thing to acknowledge Him as both Savior and Lord. An overwhelming number of Christians do not understand what is meant by Lordship. You might be thinking, "I call Him Lord, isn't that enough?"

To which my response would be, "There is a deeper relationship that God the Father desires for each of us." Oftentimes, He reveals himself through spiritual community.

MY PERSONAL LORDSHIP EXPERIENCE

It was December 1996, and for thirteen years, I had been a loyal member of an Episcopal Church with several thousand members. I had been fortunate to be the president of the men's group, a senior usher, and ordained by the Bishop as a Lay Minister and Chalice Bearer. I had attended a Cursillo weekend (spiritual retreat) and at the time was the Rector of the Ultreya group for the Cursillo program. If you had asked me if I were fully plugged into God, I would have said, "Most definitely."

However, there were areas in my life where I was not living by the biblical standard mandated by Jesus himself and would have had a tough time answering to the very issues addressed in this book.

One day, I was invited to attend a non-denominational church. During the service, I was drawn by the style of worship, so I decided to return, which I did the following Sunday. Toward the end of the service, the pastor gave an alter call asking if anyone wanted to come down and put their trust in Christ as their Savior. As he offered the invitation, I was thinking, "I've already done that."

At that very same moment, the pastor stopped mid-sentence and said, "Wait, some of you have already done that, so maybe today you need to re-confirm Him as the Lord of your life." I do not remember leaving my seat, but I found myself standing in front of the pastor along with seven other people that day. One by one, the pastor placed his hand on our shoulders and prayed for Jesus to come into our hearts and be the Lord of our Lives.

The next day, God revealed himself to me in a new way, and the spiritual blinders I had been wearing faded away. My spiritual walk took on a completely new meaning, and I experienced a change taking place in my heart. His Word seemed to jump off the pages at me with a fresh revelation of meaning.

The dots between salvation and Lordship had finally been connected, and at that moment, I no longer doubted what my status with the Lord was. Jesus was no longer just my Savior; He was my Lord. I had experienced a whole new level of spiritual revelation, one that I had been unknowingly longing for but somehow missing outside of spiritual community.

After my experience, I felt the need to speak with one of the priests at my church about what had taken place. I called and set an appointment. I knew the priest very well and openly shared my experience. I then inquired about non-denominational churches in general, asking if there was anything to fear. The priest was so gracious and offered, "I think it is wonderful that the Lord met you in another church. There is nothing to fear if the senior leader is grounded in the Gospel and under accountability. You must hear from the Lord yourself, and if you feel He is leading you down another path, then listen." I asked to be released from my membership so I could explore the possibility of joining the other church and was granted permission.

From that point on, if I believed Jesus was my Lord, wouldn't it make sense for me to search out His instruction and apply it in my life? I read the following scripture from the same sermon on the mount in Luke where Jesus instructed us on how to pray. His words cut through to my heart because I was not doing the things in which he instructed, "But why do you call Me 'Lord, Lord,' and not do the things which I say?"

However, as I read another scripture, He showed me that obedience was a result of Lordship—not a requirement. In the book of John, we learn that one of Jesus' disciples who had been with Him three years was unbelieving. It would be fair to say that Thomas didn't always do the things which Jesus instructed.

John 20:26-28

"And after eight days, His disciples were again inside, and Thomas with them. Jesus came, the doors being shut, and stood in the midst and said, 'Peace to you!' Then He said to Thomas, 'Reach your finger here and look at My hands and reach your hand here and put it into My side. Do not be unbelieving, but believing.' And Thomas answered and said to Him, 'My Lord and my God!' Jesus said to him, 'Thomas, because you have seen Me, you have believed. Blessed are those who have not seen and yet have believed.'"

In another verse, we hear from Peter as he brought a rebuke on the men of Judah in the house of Israel after the Holy Spirit had descended on the community of believers on the day of Pentecost.

Acts 2:36

"Therefore, let all the house of Israel know assuredly that God has made this Jesus, whom you crucified, both Lord and Christ."

Many scriptures reference Lordship so I encourage you to search the scriptures and go deeper in your own understanding. Pray for the Lord to grant you revelation and discernment as you read.

THOUGHT PROVOKING

> *Is Jesus the Lord of your life? If not, or if you are unsure, why not ask Christ to be the Lord of your life?*

After speaking with the priest at my church about my experience, I set an appointment with the Senior Pastor who had laid hands on me. The first question I asked, "What accountability are you under?" Initially, he was taken back at my line of questioning, but then he didn't hesitate as he explained their church structure and the men whom he was accountable to. When I expressed an interest in joining his church, he asked if I had been positively released to do so from my previous church. I stated in the affirmative, and he openly embraced my desire to explore their membership process.

Earlier, I shared that I had asked my priest about being released to explore other churches, but at that time, I didn't really understand the importance of my request. I had only asked out of respect. Later, I learned that my soon-to-be-new pastor had wanted to make sure I was spiritually covered and that his own body of believers were protected from some negative outside influence.

Many people don't understand what it means to be spiritually covered. If someone is not truly plugged into God or has unresolved issues, they are prone to jump from church to church in hopes of finding a message that fits their personal lifestyle. They often bring sinful baggage that they are not ready to deal with into those churches

Soon, after joining the new church, I joined a small home group that met on a weekly basis, studying the word and praying for one another. I learned that corporate worship was different from the worship that took place in a small group. It was much easier to share and be heard in a small group setting than when sitting in a pew on Sunday morning.

In the small group, I met two other men who expressed an interest in getting together for coffee. At our first meeting, we decided to meet weekly. Over the course of several weeks, we established a trusting relationship with one another and agreed what was said in our meetings would stay in our meetings. I soon came to realize the safety that commitment provided, and it wasn't very long before I found myself sharing intimately the painful areas of my heart. I also learned that in a small group, to hide out or ignore my problems was not easy. By joining these men at this level, I entered an area where an integral work of the ministry would be performed.

Unknowingly, I had entered a three-fold covering like our Lord, Jesus Christ. Jesus had his inner circle, which consisted of Peter, James, and John. These three were members of the twelve disciples of Jesus. The twelve were members of the 120 who met on Pentecost and received the Holy Spirit.

Without trying to orchestrate the events, the Lord had joined me to a larger group of believers, a smaller group of believers, and a one-on-one discipleship relationship with two others.

Ecclesiastes 4:9-12

"Two are better than one, Because they have a good reward for their labor. For if they fall, one will lift up his companion. But woe to him who is alone when he falls, for he has no one to help him up. Again, if two lie down together, they will keep warm; But how can one be warm alone? Though one may be overpowered by another, two can withstand him. And a threefold cord is not quickly broken."

THOUGHT PROVOKING

Do you have anyone with whom you can share the most intimate areas of your life?

My journey from that day to this has not always been one of extreme bliss. Some Christians believe that there will be no more problems once we embrace a life of Lordship. You might hear, "This is the most wonderful decision you will ever make. Your life will never be the same. You will enjoy all the fruits of the Spirit, and God will show you how much He loves you." In other words, life will be heavenly blissful.

Look, I am not denying any of these claims, but I am here to tell you the truth. Gain comes only with pain, and the Lord will continue to mold you into His image until the day you draw your last breath. For the most part, how long it will take to reach nirvana in Christ will be in direct proportion to the way you have lived your life up to the point of trusting in Christ for salvation and embracing Him as the Lord of your life.

If you have led a seemingly sin-free life, then the journey will be much more enjoyable, and you will reach that place of heavenly bliss much sooner than most. However, if you are like most of us, and the sinful nature has had control of your heart for a long time, hang on because you are in for the ride of your life.

A pastor from Denmark wrote a book called *From Pimp to Preacher.*[16] In it, he states, "Don't you know when you invite Jesus into your heart where Satan has been residing, Satan isn't going to share space with Jesus, so he flees quickly. The only problem, Satan leaves behind all of his baggage."

God will not be content until every piece of baggage Satan left behind in your heart is thrown into the refiner's fire, which will not be a comfortable process. However, at the same time, He will be building a testimony in you. That testimony will enable you to have a powerful impact in people's lives. You will be able to speak from experience into the lives of people with similar struggles as your own.

When we sincerely trust The Lord to bring us into spiritual community, He will do just that. He will join us to believers within that family whom we can relate to and learn from. Finally, He will bring us into a discipleship relationship with one or two people who are qualified to speak experientially into our lives to guide us to spiritual maturity. He will then use our testimonies in the lives of others.

We do not need to reinvent the church model. All we have to do is follow the things that Jesus did and let him be our model. If more churches followed this line of thinking, we would have less division among believers.

THOUGHT PROVOKING

How many decisions will you make in your lifetime that will have an eternal impact on your life?

---

16   *From Pimp To Precher,* by Jan Eriksen

The ultimate truth is that making a heart commitment to trust in Christ for salvation and to make Him the Lord of your life will impact you eternally. Embracing Jesus as Lord will be remembered when all else is forgotten. Your name will be written in the Book of Life.

Philippians 4:3

"And urge you also, true companion, help these women who labored with me in the gospel, with Clement also, and the rest of my fellow workers, whose names are in the Book of Life."

Revelation 20:12

"And I saw the dead, small and great, standing before God, and books were opened. And another book was opened, which is the Book of Life. And the dead were judged according to their works by the things which were written in the books."

We are all saved by grace, and the Bible tells us that nothing can take away our Salvation except blasphemy of the Holy Spirit. God will not blot out our name—He uses non-erasable ink!

John 6:37

"All that the Father gives Me will come to Me, and the one who comes to Me I will by no means cast out."

Revelation 3:5

"He who overcomes shall be clothed in white garments, and I will not blot out his name from the Book of Life,

> *but I will confess his name before My Father and before His angels."*

We are still a work in progress and have a long way to go. Please keep in mind the places and the people God plugs you into will challenge you. He is more interested in your spiritual development than allowing you to control life's circumstances. In fact, so much so that He will allow everything that comes between you and Him to be taken away, for you to receive revelation of His eternal love for you.

CHALLENGE QUESTIONS

What is gained by joining a spiritual church family?

What roll did you play in your natural family?

What roll are you called to function in within your spiritual family?

What does it mean to be equally yoked?

What does it mean to be spiritually covered?

How do you define Lordship?

What is the three-fold covering?

How would you describe your spiritual journey?

CHAPTER X

※⁓⁓⁓

STAYING PLUGGED INTO
GOD LONG TERM

"Yes, and all who desire to live godly in Christ Jesus will suffer persecution. But evil men and impostors will grow worse and worse, deceiving and being deceived." (2 Timothy 3:12-13)

Consistently staying plugged into God's power strip will be one of the hardest parts of your walk with Him. Whether you previously or just now plugged in you have God's power running through your veins, which puts a target on your soul. I would like to tell you that life will be wonderful, and everything will go your way, but I would be lying to you. The Bible tells us just the opposite.

If you give this concept some thought, you will understand that our walk with God must be that way. Society teaches us the same in the secular world from an early age. However, over the years we have deviated from the spiritual significance associated with this teaching. Instead, our tendency is to think that if we fight for a better life through the acquiring of material possessions, our lives will be happier and have significance.

Don't you think it is time we embrace the truth? We should be fighting for a life filled with spiritual significance. After all, when we die, isn't that what will really matter? What message will we impart to those we leave behind? We have all heard the saying, "I've never seen a trailer being pulled by a hearse!"

1 Timothy 6:7-10

"For we brought nothing into this world, and it is certain we can carry nothing out. And having food and clothing, with these we shall be content. But those who desire to be rich fall into temptation and a snare, and into many foolish and harmful lusts which drown men in destruction and perdition. For the love of money is a root of all kinds of evil, for which some have strayed from the faith in their greediness and pierced themselves through with many sorrows."

The proper spiritual understanding enables us to maintain balance in our lives. Our material possessions do not define our eternal livelihood. The world would have us believe that whoever dies with the most toys wins, as if life was just a game. We spend our whole lives striving to accumulate the very things that one day we will sell, give away, or pass on to our children.

From antiquity the Sphinx asked Oedipus to solve a riddle, which I will paraphrase: "What walks on all fours when it is young, two legs when it is grown and three legs when it gets old?" The answer is a man or woman—as babies we crawl on hands and knees; as we grow, we begin walking on two feet; late in life, we need the help of a cane.

Life starts out innocently enough, but then we start to age. Soon, we are on our own, exercising free will. We make some good decisions and some bad decisions. We might even be successful accumulating assets; after all, they are a way of measuring material success. However, make no mistake about it—you will not need those possessions when you die.

Most people will suffer some sort of illness before they die, and their bodies will be weakened and feeble.

THOUGHT PROVOKING

What do you think goes through a person's mind when their bodies become weak and feeble?

My Father was fifty-seven years old when he passed on to heaven. Five years before, he had had a lung removed because it contained cancer. Two years before that, he had had his voice box scraped and approximately twenty-four years before that, he had been released from the Navy after WWII weighing 120 pounds and infected with tuberculosis.

The day before he died, I sat in his hospital room along with my mother. Father was standing looking out the window onto the street below as my mother began to question God by saying, "God, why would you take my husband, but let others who are wretched live?"

Immediately, Father turned, looked her in the eye, called her by name, and said, "Enough." She and I froze and not another word was spoken.

I believe he had been reflecting on his life and having his own conversation with God. I believe he was drawing from God's power source, knowing that he would soon be joining Him for eternity.

Yes, as we reflect over our lives, we do not long for the assets accumulated or desire more junk, but rather that our lives had meaning and somehow benefited others.

THOUGHT PROVOKING

Would you agree that a meaningful life is worth fighting for?

Ephesians 6:10-12

"Finally, my brethren, be strong in the Lord and in the power of His might. Put on the whole armor of God, that you may be able to stand against the wiles of the devil. For we do not wrestle against flesh and blood, but against principalities, against powers, against the rulers of the darkness of this age, against spiritual hosts of wickedness in the heavenly places."

In the scripture above, the Apostle Paul is warning the Ephesians of the real battles they will be fighting. Paul's words were difficult to grasp back in his day, and they are still difficult to grasp in our current environments. Paul was/is speaking in spiritual terms, so unless those listening to him have revelational knowledge, his teaching makes no sense in the physical realm. Just know the Devil lies in wait for our souls.

Over the years, I have mentored many who have questioned the existence of principalities, powers, and rulers of darkness. I encouraged them to think about the history of mankind and the wars that have been fought, the blood that has been spilled. The fight between good and evil has and will be fought for generations to come. The previous conflicts took place even if we were not there to witness them. However, our lives have been greatly impacted because of those wars, some lives more so than others. Ask those who have lost loved ones or those that have lost limbs.

THOUGHT PROVOKING

Can a battle be waged in the spiritual realm and affect us physically?

A battle is being waged in the heavenly realm for our eternal souls, and our lives are being greatly impacted. Ignoring those battles does not make them go away. Many of you are facing trials and persecutions of various kinds. Putting on the armor of God in a spiritual sense protects you in the physical reality in which we live.

Ephesians 6:13-18

"Therefore take up the whole armor of God, that you may be able to withstand in the evil day, and having done all, to stand. Stand therefore, having girded your waist with truth, having put on the breastplate of righteousness, and having shod your feet with the preparation of the gospel of peace; above all, taking the shield of faith with which you will be able to quench all the fiery darts of the wicked one. And take the helmet of salvation, and the sword of the Spirit, which is the word of God, praying always with all prayer and supplication in the Spirit, being watchful to this end with all perseverance and supplication for all the saints—"

Clothing yourself in God's spiritual armor helps you undergo a change from the inside out. You become more willing to embrace the truth contained in His Word and the conviction it ignites. You begin to feel at peace in the midst of life's storms (battles). The Holy Spirit living in your heart sears your consciousness, and as you respond daily, He does a good work within you. Yes, by taking the proper spiritual action, you avoid that which is wrong and meant for your destruction. The Lord will guide you on the correct path in accordance with His will.

Hebrews 13:20-21

"Now may the God of peace who brought up our Lord Jesus from the dead, that great Shepherd of the sheep, through the blood of the everlasting covenant, make you complete in every good work to do His will, working in you what is well pleasing in His sight, through Jesus Christ, to whom be glory forever and ever. Amen."

Galatians 5:17

"For the flesh lusts against the Spirit, and the Spirit against the flesh; and these are contrary to one another, so that you do not do the things that you wish."

We will also suffer at the hand of spiritual forces that are upset that we have revelation of the true nature of Jesus Christ and His dominion over death.

John 16:33

"These things I have spoken to you that in Me you may have peace. In the world you will have

tribulation, but be of good cheer, I have overcome the world."

THOUGHT PROVOKING

Do you think that when someone trusts in Christ from the heart that life will suddenly be void of hardship?

We must overcome the inner nature, thus maintaining a balanced perspective throughout our lifetime. Let's face it—life is hard. Many of us are still suffering the consequences of our decisions and behavior before we became *Born Again* and possibly after being *Born Again*. However, there is renewed hope in Christ because He is molding us into His image, purifying us from our past, and He does not hold our sins against us.

Hebrews 8:12

"For I will be merciful to their unrighteousness, and their sins and their lawless deeds I will remember no more."'

Did you see *Deck the Halls,* a Christmas movie starring Danny DeVito and Matthew Broderick? The movie is set in a quiet, rural town where everyone knows everyone. Danny moves into town with his wife and two daughters and settles into a nice house in a suburban neighborhood. His daughters come across a website monitoring Christmas lights on Earth via satellite. Upset, they call Danny over to the computer because the lights on their house cannot be seen.

Danny's makes it his personal mission in life to light their house so it can be seen from space. However, no matter how many lights he installs, it still is not visible by satellite. He feels rejected, undervalued, and unworthy. As a result, he develops an obsession, spending every penny buying lights and decorations. Overloading his own power source, he covertly runs a cord across the street and taps into his neighbor's power. Danny was tapping into an alternative power source that was illegal. He was tapping into that power in hopes of happiness and value.

His neighbor is less than pleased by the fact that he is lighting up the whole neighborhood. Thus, a feud ensues between the two that eventually destroys the holiday and causes both families tremendous grief.

I share this story because if we are honest with ourselves, in some form or fashion we can relate to Danny's character. We long for acceptance, we want to make a difference, and we want our lights to be seen. We each have our obsessions in life and fuel those obsessions in various ways. We are constantly running on life's treadmill, not realizing that sin is dictating our destinies.

THOUGHT PROVOKING

Have you ever looked back at your life and wondered, "When did I get so far off track?"

Could it be that you unplugged from your creator and, as a result drastically veered off His chosen path for you? Have you asked yourself why life does not seem to hold the same meaning you had hoped for even after running your marathons, climbing the corporate ladder, or obtaining your material possessions?

We buy the latest and greatest gadgets, drive the nicest cars, and live in extravagant homes. We laugh at the characters in the movie, ignorant to the fact that the writers are mocking us. We are viewing an extreme example of our own everyday lives. There is a name for this type of insanity: "The rat race of life." Like a caged rat, we just keep running on the wheel in hopes of finding value and meaning.

We try to plug into all these alternate power sources for our lights to be seen from outer space. We want our houses to show up on that satellite. We want our neighbors, friends, and family to know that we have arrived and have value.

Dallas, Texas, was a great place to live after World War II. It was a big city, but small in comparison to many cities across the country. My parents settled in Dallas and began building a life. Father went to work at five every morning, and Mother raised their children and forged their social relationships. They were one of the families who fifty years ago founded a dance club that still meets in Dallas at a private Country Club. Over the course of their marriage, they developed a tremendous number of friendships.

All those friends made unique contributions to society and along the way increased in stature and wealth. They moved into nicer homes, drove nicer cars, took more trips, and were dedicated family members. They longed to provide material possessions for their children that they did not have access to growing up. Many, preparing for the later years, bought residences in retirement communities and eventually began moving into those communities.

One of those individuals brought the following observation to my attention, "My friends are pretending the life they have been living has not changed, only the scenery. They meet for cocktail hour, where they speak about their children and grandchildren, boast about their wealth, the houses they have owned, and the cars they have driven."

Of course, they were no longer living in those homes, and many could no longer drive. The reality they were facing was their purpose in life had drastically changed; they no longer seemed to be contributing to society.

As I heard about these friends, I could not help but think how sad their lives had become. Here were these well-meaning, hardworking, successful people who after World War II played a major part in kick-starting our country and developing it. Where were they now? Wasting away in a retirement community where the most important activity was evening cocktail hour and the most important conversation revolved around the homes and automobiles they own or used to own. You could say they had become spiritually stagnated. For most of their lives, they had contributed to society by advancing their wealth. Unfortunately, once they reached their senior years, all the trappings could not provide lasting happiness, peace, and joy.

THOUGHT PROVOKING

What do you think happened to these friends along life's way?

Could it be that along the path of their lives they came unplugged and lost perspective? Where was the true source of their power? It surely wasn't in their possessions. Wouldn't it make sense to embrace a relationship with the Lord, continue to stay plugged into Him, and be a role model for others?

Hear the words of the Lord's "Great Commission" found in Matthew 28:18-20,

> *"And Jesus came and spoke to them, saying, 'All authority has been given to Me in heaven and on earth. Go therefore and make disciples of all the nations, baptizing them in the name of the Father and of the Son and of the Holy Spirit, teaching them*

to observe all things that I have commanded you;
and lo, I am with you always, even to the end of the
age.' Amen."

Some of you reading this passage might be thinking, "We are all going to grow old, buddy, so who are you to judge these people?" If that thought crosses your mind as you read this, you are justified in your questioning. The intention here is not to bring judgment on myself by judging them. My intention is to remind us that we must stay plugged into God, or one day, we might end up in a stagnated state.

Many people are living in retirement homes who have not become discouraged by their surroundings. They remain plugged in by reading the bible, participating in Bible studies, and attending weekly services. Thus, they are providing a spiritual example for others in their midst and those who come to visit them. By staying plugged into the Lord, they are connected to a supernatural power source that never wears out even when their natural bodies become weaker.

Life is not about money, homes, cars, or the vacations. If we don't acknowledge the true power source and feed on it daily, one day we too will be in that retirement home, nursing our cocktails at five and talking about the money we may or may not have and the cars we own or may not own. The sad reality is our retirement home may not be as nice as my parents' friends.

The good news is this that when you stay plugged into God's power, you do not have to worry about wasting away. Instead, you can be encouraged that as your natural body is perishing, your spiritual body is preparing for a new and eternal existence in the ultimate retirement community. Do not take my word for it. Instead, read what John has to say in Revelation, the last book of the bible, where he describes this retirement community.

Revelation 21:1-2

"Now I saw a new heaven and a new earth, for the
first heaven and the first earth had passed away.
Also there was no more sea. Then I, John, saw the
holy city, New Jerusalem, coming down out of

heaven from God, prepared as a bride adorned for her husband."

THOUGHT PROVOKING

One day instead of wasting away, would you rather still be exercising your God given purpose in whatever retirement situation you find yourself?

Here is a name to make this point perfectly clear—Billy Graham. When Billy Graham stood on a platform and faced his audience, what they heard was one simple message: "You can have eternal life, Jesus loves you, and He wants to come into your heart and have a relationship with you." When people heard Billy, they went down by the thousands and stood in front of him, hungry for the power source that Billy possessed. Is it any wonder that Billy Graham ministered until he took his final breath?

You may be thinking, "No, but after all, you are talking about Billy Graham, and you, buster, are no Billy Graham." Of course, neither one of us is Billy Graham. Nevertheless, like Billy, we all have a wonderful God given purpose to fulfill here on this side of eternity. Billy knew the importance of plugging in and staying plugged into God's power source. He did not deviate from his purpose to share that message with others and was still fulfilling his purpose up until the day he died.

> *From the Blog from the Billy Graham Library's post on September 16th, 2016, we learn, "Billy Graham has made countless sacrifices for others. He gave up time with his beloved wife and children to spread the Gospel to lost people he had never met. He constantly traveled and endured hardships with media, weather and physical comfort, but that did not stop him from evangelizing."[17]*

Billy's purpose in life did not come without a price. He gave his life for that purpose, and as a result, we stand in awe of the man and his accomplishments.

---

17 *"Living Out the Gospel: Sacrifices," Billy Graham Library* (blog), September 16th, 2016, /An Example of Faith/.

It is of paramount importance to understand that by staying plugged into God, we not only learn the spiritual lessons of life, but our lives continue to have meaning until He takes us to our eternal home. We must stay plugged into Him to finish strong the race that is set before us.

2 Timothy 4:7

"I have fought the good fight, I have finished the race,
I have kept the faith."

At our core, we all want what God has to offer: His power and His divinity. Unfortunately, with all of life's difficulties, we can allow our spiritual walk with Christ to become seared to the point that we might feel like retreating to our homes, cars, and jobs to find meaning. If we allow this to happen, we run the risk of letting our spiritual power cord come unplugged. Therefore, we must keep life in balance by maintaining the proper biblical perspective through all life's circumstances.

CHALLENGE QUESTIONS

What does the following statement mean to you? "Everything worth having in life is worth fighting for."

What are the spiritual thoughts going through the mind of someone facing a terminal illness?

Are you still suffering consequences from your decisions and behavior before you became *Born Again* or after?

Have you asked yourself why life does not seem to hold the same meaning you had hoped for, even after running your marathons, climbing the corporate ladder, or obtaining your material possessions?

Have you ever looked back at your life and wondered, "When did I get so far off track spiritually?"

How are you living your life to be a role model for those coming after you?

How would you define your spiritual retirement plan?

CHAPTER XI

PLUG INTO GOD TO
RECEIVE A BLESSING

*"And let us not grow weary while doing good, for
in due season we shall reap if we do not lose
heart." (Galatians 6:9)*

To the married people reading this book, I offer the following testimony for you to share with your single friends. For the unmarried people, may the story I'm about to share offer encouragement and hope in your relational journey with our Lord.

The key to finding the right mate is to let go and allow God to prepare your heart. During this time, pray for God to show you your heart's desire for a mate. Make a list of non-negotiables. Present your list before the Lord and tell Him, "God either give me the desires of my heart or change my desires."

Psalm 37:4-5

*"Delight yourself also in the LORD, and He shall give
you the desires of your heart. Commit your way to*

the LORD, *Trust also in Him, and He shall bring it
to pass."*

God is faithful to answer prayer. In time, He will mold you in accordance with your desires knowing what is best for you. Of course, you will need to stand firm in your faith and wait on Him. Having intimate knowledge of your heart and the heart of your future mate, He knows when the time will be right to bring the two of you together. He will ultimately plug you into the right relationship.

THOUGHT PROVOKING

Do you believe that once you plug into God's power strip, He wants the best for you?

I was longing for a wife and praying for the Lord to provide just the right person. One Sunday, our church hosted a preacher from out of town. That Sunday, I happened to be sitting in the middle of the sanctuary. The preacher shared a story about how God had laid on his heart to write a letter asking God what he desired in his future wife.

He said, "Sure glad I listened and wrote the letter, or I might not have recognized the woman God introduced me to two weeks later." Pointing to a woman in the audience he continued, "May I introduce my wife? We have been happily married for twenty years. God longs to grant us the desires of our heart. Isn't it time you write down those desires?"

Immediately, I rolled my eyes up to the ceiling and said, "Why do I have to write you a letter, like you don't know what I want?" I would like to add that my expression was quite snide. Suddenly, the sanctuary grew silent, and there was no response in my sub-conscious mind. After a few minutes I felt convicted about my response, I thought, "All right, I'll write down my heart's desires."

Well, being a stubborn male at the time, instead of writing a letter, I bulleted my desires for a wife on a 3" x 5" card. The following is a replica of my original list:

Non-Negotiables

- 5'- 2" to 5'- 3" – Lord I've always been drawn to shorter women.

- Green or blue eyes that resonate Christ.
- Golden highlights, like my old dog Brandy.
- Someone who is financially stable and not out for money.
- I want her to have tire marks on her back. She needs to have been through tough times spiritually and as a result was strengthened in her Christian character.
- Not contentious. I do not want to fight anymore. I would rather go to my grave single.
- Must be trustworthy and loyal.

From that day forward I began to pray over my list embracing the earlier quoted Psalm 37:4, *"Delight yourself also in the Lord, and He shall give you the desires of your heart."*

A few days after crafting my list, I experienced an encounter with the Lord that challenged me further. In my prayer time one morning, a still, small voice whispered into my inner ear, "When do you kiss the bride?"

I remember thinking, "Why in the world am I having that thought? I'm not even dating anyone."

After pondering the question, I responded, "I guess after the marriage officiant announces, 'I pronounce you man and wife, and now you may kiss the bride.'"

There was an eerie silence in the room, and after several minutes had passed that same voice said, "Well?"

I knew the Holy Spirit had offered a challenge. Processing His question over the next few weeks, I concluded that the Lord wanted to use the challenge to protect me from myself, given my propensity in the past to enter into a physical relationship with those I dated.

I also reasoned that if the Lord truly was behind the challenge, then any woman I entertained having a relationship with would understand and appreciate the reason I did not want to kiss. If not, then their lack of understanding would be a sign that she might not be the woman God had selected for me.

A peace engulfed me and solidified my commitment, so I made a covenant with the Lord determining not to kiss a woman romantically again until after being married.

In my first book, *Freedom from S.I.N.,* I share a concept about "Relational Practice Rounds." My premise was that we all practice sports without objection, but with the opposite sex, we tend to dive right into relationships investing our emotions, often times out of selfish desire. I encouraged those reading to enjoy the relationship journey, get to know one another's heart, and learn how to treat one another with respect. Any relationship that doesn't work out is just a *practice round* for that one special person the Lord would introduce into their lives.

> *"The biggest decision you will make in your life is the decision to trust Jesus Christ for your salvation. The second biggest decision most of us will make is choosing the person we will marry and spend the rest of our days with here on earth.*[18]

Sixteen years passed since making the non-kissing commitment to the Lord, and my spiritual journey had taken me to Africa, South America, and Cuba. During those mission trips, I was exposed to a different side of the world and learned compassion. So many people around the world are oppressed and, like all of us, are longing to fill the God-size hole in their hearts. The stories I could tell are numerous, but I will save those for another writing.

Around this time, I was faced with some false accusations at the church I was attending. Despair and disappointment engulfed me. I got the sense that the enemy's attacks were intended to get me to take offense and leave the church. I wasn't feeling much love at the time, but I did not waver. In each circumstance, I was facing I knew where all the relational skeletons were buried, and I was in good standing with the Lord. In fact, I had a conversation with the Lord letting Him know that I wasn't going anywhere unless He moved me. I also knew most of the churches around town. Where would I go anyway?

Two weeks after having the conversation with the Lord, our pastor invited an Anglican priest to preach at our church. He was starting a *spirit filled* church in central Dallas. As he was being introduced, a shock went through my system. He and I had played football together in junior high school. After the service we embraced and caught up on life. My pastor had been asked to do a prophetic teaching at the priest's new church, so I began volunteering as well.

The next three months were life inspiring. I connected with old friends and felt an overwhelming amount of love. At the end of the sum-

---

18   Lawrence Luby, *Freedom from S.I.N.* (Dallas: HIS Publishing, 2008),224.

mer, I learned that the spiritual core of the church was based on three streams: Spirit, Sacraments, and Scripture. Immediately upon reading their foundational statement a voice whispered, "This is your new spiritual home."

I listed the prayers I had been praying and set an appointment with my pastor. Before entering his office, I spoke to the Lord, "If you are moving me to a new church, then you will need to tell him."

I didn't need my pastor's permission, but I did need the Lord's blessing. If the Lord were really speaking to me, I knew he would confirm my decision using my current pastor. I began the meeting by sharing my prayers and asked, "What do you think about me joining the Anglican church?"

My pastor looked to the side and was silent for a few minutes before he looked me squarely in the eye and said, "I think it is great you have reconnected with old friends. I don't have a check in my spirit at all."

By "check in his spirit" he was referring to his inner spirit's connection to the Holy Spirit. We explored this concept in chapter six.

I made the transition and will not bore you with the details. I will mention that I resumed my prior service as a chalice bearer at my new church and served at a funeral one Saturday morning. After the service, I was asked to join the family for a luncheon they were hosting. At that lunch, I met a lady, and we talked about our lives, our pain, and our desires. She shared that her mother had recently passed. I saw a tear drop from one of her green eyes (see my list) and the way the light was shining her eye looked like an emerald.

I shared my decision not to kiss a woman romantically before marriage.

She then responded, "You know that is interesting. All the guys want to kiss, but kissing is intimate and not to be taken lightly."

I thought to myself, "I can't believe this woman isn't married. I need to ask her to coffee."

Not wanting to ask for her number at the lunch, I exited the house and waited in my car for her to leave. After several minutes, I concluded she wasn't leaving and started my car. At that moment, she came out of the house and walked right up to my window. I asked if she would like to have coffee sometime, and without hesitation she said, "Sure, let me give you my number." I nervously dropped my phone and then entered her number.

Starting to walk off, she paused, pointed her finger at me, and said, "And no kissing!"

As I put my hand on the gear shift that little voice whispered, "She is the one."

Our first coffee lasted three hours. After our visit, I was walking her to her car, and I casually asked, "By the way, how tall are you?"

She said, "five foot two."

Silently, I pumped my fist and said, "Yes!"

The next day, I received a voice mail message from her, "Larry, please call me I have been to the doctor, and I really need to speak with you."

After listening to the message, I thought, "Wow, I just met this woman, and now she is going to die on me."

I returned the call, and she told me, "Well, I went to the doctor today, and they measured me. I must have grown one half inch. I'm now five foot two and half."

You can imagine my shock. I looked to the sky and said, "Lord, you really do have a sense of humor."

She called me one week later to ask me a question, "Does your hair get lighter during the summer?"

I looked down at the hair on my arm which is blond and said, "Well, I have a blond complexion, but at this stage of life, all you're going to see is my gray hair."

We both laughed, and she said, "Well mine does. Do you mind if I get a few more golden highlights?"

I just about fell out of my chair, and I sensed the Lord smiling down, proud of Himself that He was being so specific in granting the desires of my heart.

I had waited sixteen years, and during that time, I had male friends question how I could remain celibate and not even kiss. My response was always, "I've made that mistake before and don't plan on going around that mountain again. Besides, once I meet her, I won't be pissing and moaning about not having her. I will be ecstatic that I am with her!"

We have been together as of this writing for eight years, and the Lord fulfilled every item on my list. I want to encourage anyone reading who is lonely and praying for a mate. Write down your desires, pray over them, and amend the list until you can honestly say, "I would rather go to my grave than compromise the items on my list." Then turn the list over to the Lord and let go.

THOUGHT PROVOKING

Wouldn't it make sense to write down your desires when making other life decisions? Some examples might be which school to attend, which vocation to choose, how to raise children, or what you want for your grandchildren.

Use these lists as failsafes, knowing that the Lord does not compromise in His answers to our prayers. He will either grant your desires or change your desires. But when you finally know the longing of your heart and have been prepared, He will act in accordance with what is best for you.

The Lord is faithful, but everything happens on His time schedule, not ours. It might not take sixteen years for the Lord to ready your heart for that one special person or provide direction about the course of your life. Regardless how long His process takes you will be blessed by the choice He has for you.

Men, when the time is right, you will awake
like Adam and find your Eve,

And, ladies, you will awake to find your Adam.

CHALLENGE QUESTION

How many of your relationships have ended in disappointment because of unmet expectations?

What do you think the Lord was teaching you through those relationships?

Do you know the desires of your heart?

Do you believe that God can introduce you to that one person He has set aside for you?

If you are single, what is keeping you from listing your non-negotiables when it comes to a future mate?

Are you willing to wait on the Lord to receive His best?

Shouldn't you trust the Lord for direction with every major decision in life?

CHAPTER XII

ULTREYA - ONWARD

"Not that I have already attained, or am already perfected, but I press on, that I may lay hold of that for which Christ Jesus has also laid hold of me. Brethren, I do not count myself to have apprehended, but one thing I do, forgetting those things which are behind and reaching forward to those things which are ahead, I press toward the goal for the prize of the upward call of God in Christ Jesus." (Philippians 3:12-14)

Ultreya, meaning onward, is a word derived from the original Latin. I pray that all who read this book will be inspired to press onward and upward in Christ Jesus. My desire as I wrote the book was to encourage people to deal with personal issues, get in touch with God's purpose for their lives, and finish strong the journey that lies ahead.

"Onward Christian Soldiers" was written in 1865 by Sabine Baring-Gould, a Roman Catholic priest. The song has provided encouragement and strength over the years to those enduring hardships. The lyrics are based on New Testament references such as 2 Timothy 2:3, "You therefore must endure hardship as a good soldier of Jesus Christ." As Christians we are challenged to become soldiers for Christ and to stand strong knowing that Christ is our royal Master, especially when facing the challenges of life.

Verse 1
Onward, Christian soldiers, marching as to war,
With the cross of Jesus going on before.
Christ, the royal Master, leads against the foe;
Forward into battle see His banners go!

Verse 4
Crowns and thrones may perish, kingdoms rise and wane,
But the church of Jesus constant will remain.
Gates of hell can never against that church prevail;
We have Christ's own promise, and that cannot fail.

Ultimately, we will all be members of one church—God's eternal church in heaven. Onward we all go in life, but God's desire has always been for us to walk in unity as believers. Therefore, plugging into a scripturally sound church on this side of eternity that embraces God's divine nature makes sense. In so doing, we press onward toward our eternal home with the Savior in relationship with other believers here on earth.

Ephesians 1:22-23

"And He put all things under His feet and gave Him to be head over all things to the church, which is His body, the fullness of Him who fills all in all."

Unfortunately, the enemy has divided us across denominational lines. If the truth were known, many denominations believe they alone have all the answers to God's eternal kingdom. The problem with this way of thinking is that it is not biblical. No one has all the answers.

Romans 3:9-12

"What then? Are we better than they? Not at all. For we have previously charged both Jews and Greeks that they are all under sin. As it is written:

'There is none righteous, no, not one;

There is none who understands;

There is none who seeks after God.

They have together become unprofitable;

There is none who does good, no, not one.'"

God never intended for the church to be split. However, He understands that men and women are different and will usually flock to others like themselves. We should give proper credit to the men who started various denominational movements, such as John Wesley, George Whitefield, Martin Luther, John Calvin, John Knox, and others. These individuals were all scholars in their times and no doubt heard from God. They all embraced the true meaning of Ultreya by pressing onward. As a result, we have many spiritual families to choose from.

Culturally, people are different and are attracted to various denominations based on experience and belief. My hope is that the various denominations will embrace the fact that if they truly profess to be Christ followers they are connected to God's power source and connected to one another to achieve the same goal: to make disciples for Christ.

Often, people will change churches or cross denominational lines when they are offended, want to feel better, or possibly justify a certain behavior. Recently, I heard a radio broadcast by Charles Stanley who stated, "People want to sin without the consequence." Well, in the story I related earlier in this book about the men in my former Episcopal group, we had found a church where we were given permission to sin seemingly without consequence.

Unfortunately, in many churches, this thought process continues because there is little or no accountability. Many churches are being led by strong, entrepreneurial leaders who had a vision from God. Many of those leaders are well meaning and lead their congregations accordingly. Nevertheless, there have been those that were not well meaning and led their congregations astray.

Examples are found in the tragic stories of men like Jim Jones in Jonestown, Guyana, and David Koresh in Waco, Texas. We could also mention the polygamist sects that are leading many men and women to an eternity separated from the Father. People long to plug into a power source and so often plug into an individual or a group embracing an ideal. However, in the examples cited, the power source was demonic, dangerous, and ended in the destruction of souls.

These examples are extreme, but I offer them to get your attention because many ministries and churches today are leading people astray. The problem is that if those congregations are not plugged in correctly to God, the members are at risk. Therefore, you need to know whom you are plugging into. Ask questions, pray for the Lord's guidance, and be open to the leading of the Holy Spirit.

- To what spiritual doctrine does your congregation ascribe?
- Does the congregation follow the Apostle's Creed?
- Does the leadership believe that Jesus is the Son of God and embrace that salvation comes only through trusting in His death and resurrection?
- Are Jesus Christ and the Holy Spirit at the center of every aspect of their ministry?
- Are the pastors and elders making it perfectly clear that members of the church should be unplugging from the world and its lusts and plugging into God through the Holy Scriptures?

1 Corinthians 15:3-4

"For I delivered to you first of all that which I also received: that Christ died for our sins according to the Scriptures, and that He was buried, and that He rose again the third day according to the Scriptures,"

If the church you are attending can't answer these questions in the affirmative, then you might need to unplug and pray for the Lord to lead you to His desired community. God will bring you into right relationships if you will be patient and allow Him to work in your heart. He is not intentionally going to put any of us in harm's way.

We have looked at how God plugs us into others through discipleship that is initiated when God puts someone in our lives who is qualified to be our spiritual guide. The Lord introduces us to these chosen people when He knows we are ready to deal with the tough issues of life.

These individuals do not speak from something they learned in a book; instead, they speak from their own life experiences. Their testimonies will be born out of pain and suffering and will become a beacon of hope in your life as you develop an empirical connection with them.

The enemy's sole intent and purpose is to divide the house of the Lord by defiling our relationships. When you learn to trust people whom God puts in your life, you gain a renewed confidence that you too can make it through tough times. Through this type of Holy Spirit connection, your heart will be touched in such a way that it alters the course of your life.

1 Peter 5:8-9

> "Be sober, be vigilant because your adversary the devil walks about like a roaring lion, seeking whom he may devour. Resist him, steadfast in the faith, knowing that the same sufferings are experienced by your brotherhood in the world."

THOUGHT PROVOKING

I ask, if you were Satan, and you wanted to disrupt God's order, what plan would you employ?

Our culturally diverse society would have us believe the opposite of the truth. One of our spiritual enemy's characteristics is deception, so we must remember He is sneaky. We do not give him enough credit in the deception department. He uses our own hearts to deceive us, not to mention our relationships, families, and other people around us. The devil is alive and on the prowl, and we have been ignorant for too long!

Living a life in which Jesus is Lord is not to be taken lightly. Unfortunately, we live in a world where many Christians profess to be *Born Again* believers, but few profess to be living a life totally committed to Jesus Christ.

THOUGHT PROVOKING

Do you think society has distorted the thinking within many of the mainstream churches so that only a few congregations really hear the whole truth from the pulpit?

The message of the Gospel becomes diluted with cultural codicils. Some people even use the excuse that the Bible was written too long ago and must be altered to meet the current time and events. One example is the replacement of anything appearing masculine. We have compromised God's written word, diluting it in order not to offend anyone in particular.

God's word, as written in the Bible, is meant to be a guide for our Christian living. It is the manual on how to live a fulfilled life. The gospel must be presented in full force, which can only be done when we model the love, grace, and mercy of God and acknowledge Jesus Christ as the source of our salvation. The gospel then comes alive in the hearts of believers by the power of the Holy Spirit.

Therefore, based on God's Word, when you trust Christ for salvation and ask Him into your heart, suddenly (possibly without feeling anything), you have just plugged into God's power strip. The Bible tells us at that moment the Holy Spirit enters the heart, we are sealed for all eternity. The Holy Spirit allows the power of God to flow throughout our heart, soul, and mind. He begins to do a work in your system effecting a heart change that begins molding you into His image. Of course, the process continues until the day you breathe your last.

Ephesians 1:13-14

"In Him you also trusted, after you heard the word of truth, the gospel of your salvation, in whom also, having believed, you were sealed with the Holy Spirit of promise, who is the guarantee of our inheritance until the redemption of the purchased possession, to the praise of His glory."

I witnessed an example of how God works in the heart of a believer on a mission trip. I had the privilege of traveling to Lusaka, Zambia, with a team to host a leadership conference for African pastors. One of the men traveling with us had Lou Gehrig's disease; he was only forty-eight years old.

He had built a career and become a successful executive who owned several companies, sat on numerous boards, and by his own admission, thought he had the world in the palm of his hand. Yet, in his early forties, he entered into a dark period of life. His marriage was in trouble, his youngest daughter had an eating disorder, and he was angry at everything and everyone.

Fortunately, his daughter entered a 12-step program for her addiction, and as a result of what God did in her life, God got the attention of everyone in her family. Out of her darkness, the family experienced a spiritual healing process. Sadly, during the same period, something was taking place within her father's body; he was dying physically. However, by the time his disorder was diagnosed, his spiritual man had been birthed and matured to such a degree that his life took on a whole new meaning.

Knowing his time to die could come at any moment, he began each day spending time with Christ. He started journaling to his heavenly Father and his family. He scheduled time for friends, knowing that business could wait. He realized there were actually flowers to stop and smell. He started drinking the good wine instead of saving it for later.

He constructed a whole list outlining how he was going to live his life and began to share that list with others. He decided not to take anything for granted but gave thanks to God for every day he was alive. He got revelation of what it really meant to be *Born Again* in the Spiritual sense. He realized the more his mortal body was decaying the more his spiritual man was becoming stronger.

He longed to join the Kingdom Jesus spoke of in Heaven. The closer he came to a physical death the more alive he became in the Spirit. Out of his hardship and brokenness, he found God's Kingdom on Earth.

To date, he has led more men and women in their quest to spiritual truth than nearly anyone else I know. By plugging into God's power source, his life became a living testimony. He modeled Ultreya throughout his life by pushing onward against great odds.

THOUGHT PROVOKING

Have you experienced a distinct revelation that brought you to the point of plugging into God?

If not, I pray that you will experience a revelation that burns your consciousness in such a way that your life will never be the same. I don't pray that you would contract a disease like my friend, but that God would reach deep within your heart and grab your attention.

We read in scripture that the Apostle Paul came to understand this concept better than anyone. Paul was originally, Saul of Tarsus, a Pharisee, on a mission from the High Priest to eradicate the followers of Jesus.

Acts 9:1-2

"Then Saul, still breathing threats and murder against the disciples of the Lord, went to the high priest and asked letters from him to the synagogues of Damascus, so that if he found any who were of the Way, whether men or women, he might bring them bound to Jerusalem."

However, one day on a journey to Damascus, Paul had a revelation from the Lord that not only saved his soul from hell but also transformed him into one of the strongest servants for Christ who has ever lived. He learned how to plug into God.

Acts 9:3-6

"As he journeyed he came near Damascus, and suddenly a light shone around him from heaven. Then he fell to the ground and heard a voice saying to him, 'Saul, Saul, why are you persecuting Me?' And he said, 'Who are You, Lord?' Then the Lord said, 'I am Jesus, whom you are persecuting. It is hard for you to kick against the goads.' So he, trembling and astonished, said, 'Lord, what do You want me to do?' Then the Lord said to him, 'Arise and go into the city, and you will be told what you must do.'"

What happened as a result of Paul's experience? He became one of the strongest advocates for Jesus Christ who has ever walked the earth, wrote thirteen epistles (some say fourteen), founded seven churches, and trained up many disciples for the Lord, including Timothy and Titus.

Based on what we know of Paul's life, we can agree that he fully understood the covering provided when a person truly plugs into God the Father, God the Son, and God the Holy Spirit—the triune Creator of the universe. However, Paul remained humble, for he knew well his sin still remained. But he embraced the concept of Ultreya, and we are blessed by his spiritual journey today as we read the Word.

Romans 7:24-25

"O wretched man that I am! Who will deliver me from this body of death? I thank God—through Jesus Christ our Lord! So then, with the mind I myself serve the law of God, but with the flesh the law of sin."

In Closing

The Holy Spirit brings revelation of God's Word. When we sincerely invite the Holy Spirit into our hearts through faith, we are saved by grace and become plugged into God's power strip. His Word comes to life in our hearts through the scriptures as God speaks to us. God begins to reveal the purposes He placed on our hearts before birth, and our lives take on new meaning.

As believers, when we remain focused on God through spiritual connection, we continue to join with other believers, and our spiritual family expands, even across denominational lines. We are the individuals who collectively make up the Christian Church. We are the ones who have embraced Ultreya by moving onward and upward.

We come to understand what it means to be *Plugged into God*, to His eternal kingdom, to His power strip. Therefore, one day, we will join our Lord in His eternal Kingdom, which He calls paradise.

Revelation 2:7

"...To him who overcomes I will give to eat from the tree of life, which is in the midst of the Paradise of God."

Are You Plugged Into God's Power?

To purchase other books by
Lawrence Luby, visit the publisher's website
www.hispublish.com

www.ingramcontent.com/pod-product-compliance
Lightning Source LLC
Chambersburg PA
CBHW050824090426
42738CB00021B/3473